Originally trained as a primary school teacher, Alison Harris has been in resourcing and training those involved in all aspects of children's ministry was the Adviser for Children's Ministry in Chester Diocese for nearly nine y___ ___ ____ worked with BRF for two years as the *Barnabas* representative for the North of England. Her particular interests and concerns include encouraging churches to recognize and take seriously children's spiritual and faith development, opening up the Bible to children, engaging children in worship, young children's spirituality and developing provision to foster this, and the challenge of creating churches as truly all-age communities. Alison recently completed a Master of Theology degree, for which her in-depth research concerned the interface between sacred stories and young children. Having trained at the Queen's Foundation for Ecumenical Theological Education in Birmingham, she is now a curate in Chester Diocese.

Important information

Photocopy permission

The right to photocopy material in *Praise and Play* is granted for the pages that contain the photocopying clause, 'Reproduced with permission from *Praise and Play* published by BRF 2009 (978 1 84101 563 7)', so long as reproduction is for use in a teaching situation by the original purchaser. The right to photocopy material is not granted for anyone other than the original purchaser without written permission from BRF.

The Copyright Licensing Agency (CLA)

If you are resident in the UK and you have a photocopying licence with the Copyright Licensing Agency (CLA), please check the terms of your licence. If your photocopying request falls within the terms of your licence, you may proceed without seeking further permission. If your request exceeds the terms of your CLA licence, please contact the CLA direct with your request. Copyright Licensing Agency, 90 Tottenham Court Road, London W1T 4LP. Telephone 020 7631 5555; fax 020 7631 5500; email cla@cla.co.uk; website www.cla.co.uk. The CLA will provide photocopying authorization and royalty fee information on behalf of BRF.

BRF is a Registered Charity (No. 233280)

Text copyright © Alison Harris 2009
Illustrations copyright © Charlie Fowkes 2009
The author asserts the moral right
to be identified as the author of this work

Published by
The Bible Reading Fellowship
15 The Chambers, Vineyard
Abingdon OX14 3FE
United Kingdom
Tel: +44 (0)1865 319700
Email: enquiries@brf.org.uk
Website: www.brf.org.uk

ISBN 978 1 84101 563 7
First published 2009
10 9 8 7 6 5 4 3 2 1 0
All rights reserved

Acknowledgments
Unless otherwise stated, scripture quotations are taken from the Contemporary English Version of the Bible published
by HarperCollins Publishers, copyright © 1991, 1992, 1995 American Bible Society.

Scripture quotations taken from the Holy Bible, New International Version, copyright © 1973, 1978, 1984 by
International Bible Society, are used by permission of Hodder & Stoughton Publishers, a division of Hodder Headline
Ltd. All rights reserved. 'NIV' is a registered trademark of International Bible Society. UK trademark number 1448790.

Scripture quotations taken from The New Revised Standard Version of the Bible, Anglicized Edition, copyright © 1989,
1995 by the Division of Christian Education of the National Council of the Churches of Christ in the USA, are used by
permission. All rights reserved.

Scriptures quoted from the Good News Bible published by The Bible Societies/HarperCollins Publishers Ltd, UK ©
American Bible Society 1966, 1971, 1976, 1992, used with permission.

Songs taken from *Come and Praise: Beginning* by Jo Daykin, published by Pearson Education Ltd, are used by kind
permission of the publishers.

A catalogue record for this book is available from the British Library

Printed in Singapore by Craft Print International Ltd

Praise and Play

Worshipping with under-fives

Alison Harris

Acknowledgments

I am deeply indebted to the *Praise and Play* congregations (children and adults) from St Chad's Church, Irby (Wirral), St Thomas' Church, Stockton Heath (Warrington), and All Saints' Church, Saughall (Chester), who have been such an important part of my journey into the whole area of young children and worship. I am particularly grateful to the *Praise and Play* group in Saughall, who were so willing to be the pilot group for the sessions outlined in this book. I would also like to thank Carol Ridley, who first introduced me to the concept of *Praise and Play* over twelve years ago, without whom all this may never have happened.

The work in this book has been adapted from work submitted for an MTh degree with Chester University.

Preface

A few years ago, two interesting conversations occurred with young children around Christmas time. During Advent, we include on our *Praise and Play* 'focus table' a beany lion and a calf (recalling the prophecy in Isaiah 11:6). As we were setting up the table, one child was adamant that we should not put the lion and the calf together because the lion would eat the calf—it's obvious! I wondered out loud for a moment, 'I wonder if the lion and the calf can *ever* live together?' to which Ryan, aged nearly four, whispered to his grandfather, 'They can in God's house'.

The second conversation happened on Christmas Eve, when we had a special *Praise and Play* service in which we set up the Christmas crib. After the service, we left an aesthetically arranged crib scene as we went into the adjacent room for refreshments. Later I came out to see Jack, aged about three, completely absorbed in rearranging the scene. Everything was being crammed into the stable: Mary, Joseph, Jesus, shepherds, sheep, wise men, camels, the cow and the donkey. I knelt down by his side, watching what he was doing. In response to my interest, he said, 'I want everyone to see baby Jesus.'

Here were two profound and privileged moments with young children, which serve to remind us that, as young as they are, children are spiritual beings. My hope and my prayer for Ryan and Jack, and for countless others like them, is that their spirituality will grow and flourish into a lively and life-giving faith in God through Jesus Christ. This book offers one way in which we can seek to nurture that spirituality through worship. It arises from over twelve years of experience and involvement in *Praise and Play* services in a number of different contexts. The twelve sessions have all been tried and tested with a *Praise and Play* group.

Contents

Foreword 8

Thinking about worship 9

Introducing *Praise and Play* 11

Unpacking *Praise and Play* 14

Storytelling materials 20

Session 1:   Jesus is born 22

Session 2:   The wise men visit Jesus 26

Session 3:   Jesus and his disciples 29

Session 4:   The good shepherd 32

Session 5:   Jesus blesses little children 36

Session 6:   Jesus heals an older woman and a young girl 40

Session 7:   The man with a hundred sheep 44

Session 8:   Jesus calms a storm 47

Session 9:   Jesus feeds a great crowd..50

Session 10:   Jesus and Zacchaeus..53

Session 11:   Jesus appears to Mary Magdalene 56

Session 12:   Jesus is with us all the time 60

              Templates 63

              Bibliography 74

Foreword

As a practitioner and parent, it is my belief that children have a place in church and should be nurtured from birth, rather than just being entertained until they are older and therefore able to 'understand'. It is important that they are encouraged to be members of the church community, enabled to worship with their family and friends and helped to feel that they are part of something bigger. Children should not only be recognized as learners but should also be valued for their ability to teach others. We must therefore ensure that they can explore the stories of the Bible for themselves in a way that is relevant and gives them the opportunity to share their thoughts, beliefs and opinions. It's not a case of simply telling children stories; we must also listen to what they say.

It is refreshing to hear Alison promote and enthuse about the virtues of play and its place within worship. All too often, the emphasis for young children is on craft—and play, which is a big part of children's lives, is overlooked. Children learn so much through play; it engages children of all ages and abilities, giving them the opportunity to explore the Bible for themselves in a way that is safe.

Work with young children and their families is particularly under-resourced and is an area of ministry that people find difficult to engage with, so it is fantastic to have such an easy-to-use resource to help groups with some ready-made outlines for sessions. The general information about where, when, why and how is an invaluable tool to help groups to get started and think about what they do. It is also really useful for established groups who want to review or change what they are doing.

Alison's knowledge and experience have been indispensable in producing this resource that values children, their knowledge, their gifts and their talents.

Ellie Wilson
Under 5s Children's Adviser, Diocese of Wakefield

Thinking about worship

Why do we worship?

Gathering together to worship God has been an important part of Christian discipleship and witness since the earliest days of the Church. Corporate worship—gathering together for worship—is important for our spiritual growth. It reflects much of what we hold to be important as the body of Christ, and it shapes us as we continue to grow in discipleship and in ministry and mission within our own communities and the wider world. In corporate worship we praise God (hymns, prayers and psalms), we hear his story and reflect on its message for us today (readings and sermon), we confess our shortcomings and receive pardon so that we can make a fresh start (confession and absolution), we share with God our concerns for the world (prayers of intercession), we proclaim together the essentials of what we believe (the statement of faith or creed) and, at the end, we are sent out, strengthened to live out our calling beyond the church doors in the coming week (the blessing and dismissal). If the service is Holy Communion, we share in the great prayer of thanksgiving and receive the bread and wine.

Corporate worship, however, has often been seen very much as an adult domain and not appropriate for children generally, much less very young children. We might try to keep young children amused and occupied in worship, but it is as if that is the most we can expect until they are old enough really to understand and participate in it themselves.

Too young to worship?

Many churches consciously try to develop ways of encouraging young children to feel comfortable and accepted when they come to church, and that is important. But this book is about doing more than that; this book is about helping young children to worship. Some people will be very sceptical about this. After all, young children cannot be still for very long, young children cannot read, young children do not 'understand' about God, young children cannot... the list could go on! Although these factors might seem to be a crucial part of our corporate worship, they are by no means essential. Are young children such 'empty vessels' in the worship stakes?

A prime time to engage in corporate worship!

It is easy to assume that participation in worship calls for a fairly sophisticated understanding of language, both spoken and written, but worship is more than words. In corporate worship there *are* words, both said and sung, but there can also be movement, drama, silence, actions, symbols and ritual, all of which can resonate with young children. Indeed, far from being 'empty vessels', young children have many of the basic ingredients necessary for worship.

- Young children are spiritual beings. They are created in the image of God (Genesis 1:27), 'knitted together' by God in their mother's womb (Psalm 139:13, NIV). In fact, if spirituality is an innate and universal dimension of what it means to be human, then spirituality will not just be *present* in young children, but may even be at its most intense in early childhood before it has been overlaid with other ideas and experiences.
- Many young children, even those who have not experienced a religious environment, have a sense of God before they are three years old.
- Young children 'make sense' of experiences intuitively through their senses and through their spirits before they can articulate their understanding and feelings in language. They know intuitively much more than they can express in words.
- Children are profoundly open to moments of awe and wonder.
- They are naturally spontaneous and are not inhibited about displaying expressions of joy, enthusiasm, excitement, sadness, care and concern.
- They appreciate and want to join in with familiar patterns, rhythms and rituals.
- They have an effective memory for actions: they will copy, join in with and want to repeat them.
- They love stories.

- They love drama and play.
- Young children know what it is to be in relationship: they are born into a relational situation, and a sense of being in relationship both with God and with other people is an essential part of corporate worship.
- They appreciate symbol (they use symbols in their play all the time), as long as one of the parts of the symbolic representation is familiar to them.
- They have a natural desire to participate.
- They love to celebrate.
- They can be completely absorbed in the things that engage them.

In addition, young children are naturally curious, they are keen to make sense of the world around them, and they are open and eager to learn new language. Rather than thinking that children need to acquire certain skills or reach a certain level of maturity or understanding before they can participate in corporate worship, we should consider these early years as a prime time for encouraging them in corporate worship by harnessing the capacities that are already present. The early years are widely recognized as crucially important for the development of all kinds of human capacities and abilities, so why not develop their spiritual capacities through corporate worship?

Introducing Praise and Play

Imagine the scene… While some babies sit on adults' knees, five or six older pre-school children search the back of the church for various hidden items. Once the objects are found, the children come to the front, some walking slowly, holding their item very carefully, others running up the aisle with great eagerness. They all place their items on the special table at the front. The table doesn't always end up looking tidy or artistically arranged, but it is more important for the children to feel that this is their special space. Then, everyone watches and listens expectantly as the candle is lit and the same words—repeated each week—are spoken: 'We light this candle to help us remember that we have come to spend a special time with God and a special time with each other.'

So begins a *Praise and Play* service—a regular midweek service for pre-school children and their carers. In this group there can be two-week-old babies, toddlers, mums, dads, grandparents, child minders and even friends who are just visiting for the day, but all have come 'to spend a special time with God and a special time with each other'.

A number of churches have a regular midweek service for pre-school children and their carers, and many find that such a service is a really positive way of offering something very important to young families. It provides:

✪ A safe, non-threatening opportunity for people to bring their babies and toddlers to church, especially those for whom church is a new and probably intimidating place.
✪ A special time for children and their carers to share together.
✪ A means of helping and encouraging parents to begin to fulfil the promises they made for their child if he or she was baptized as an infant.
✪ A means of helping and encouraging carers to be faith nurturers for their children by giving them ideas and tools for bringing elements of the Christian faith into their homes. How often has a parent said later, 'We've been singing that song all week'!

All these factors are important in the *Praise and Play* service, but such midweek provision for young children is rarely regarded as 'proper' worship. However, there is a conscious intention to develop *Praise and Play* as authentic corporate worship; its shape mirrors the fourfold pattern of worship that is widely used within the Christian community (gathering, word, response, conclusion/sending), but at the same time it recognizes the gifts and the needs that young children bring to worship. Furthermore, although *Praise and Play* may initially be intended to minister to the spiritual needs of young children, experience shows that it also ministers to the spiritual needs of the adults who come, many of whom may be new to corporate worship themselves.

Getting started

Where should it happen?

Praise and Play should take place preferably in the church, especially if that is where most of your church's corporate worship happens. Some people may be aghast at the thought of a service for pre-school children happening in church, but it is a wonderful opportunity to reassure young families that the church and worship really are for them as well. Parents are often intimidated by the church building. 'Coming to church' might be a completely new experience for them, or they might have fearful memories of what church was like when they were children, so the thought of bringing their young children arouses still more anxiety.

Try to create a warm and positive environment within the church. Use a specific section of the church, such as a side chapel, or move furniture to mark off a special area (for example, rearrange chairs to form a semicircle around the altar or Communion table, or at the foot of the chancel steps). Young children feel reassured by the security of a defined space. Make sure the carpet is clean. You could also put down cushions or kneelers for children (and maybe some adults) to sit on. Arrange for the heating to be turned on in good time.

When should it happen?

You need to allow at least an hour for *Praise and Play*: the worship lasts for 20–25 minutes, and then you need time for activities and refreshments, free play and a chat. Do some neighbourhood research and avoid times when other events are happening in your locality for pre-school children. In setting the time, take account of the fact that carers may need to take older siblings to and from school.

Be wary of tacking *Praise and Play* on to an existing parent and toddler group. Even though some parent and toddler groups meet on church premises, they may have, at best, a very loose connection with the church. Adding on *Praise and Play* without the substantial agreement of those who already go to the group can generate an attitude of suspicion and resentment. However, existing parent and toddler groups and other pre-school provision can be good places to advertise *Praise and Play*.

How often should it happen?

Frequency depends on the availability of people to lead the worship and be involved in the organization. In some churches, *Praise and Play* happens weekly; this helps to build a greater sense of community and encourages people to form a 'habit' of regular worship, but it does require a team of people able to commit themselves to weekly attendance. Some churches organize *Praise and Play* services fortnightly or monthly, and some just at special festival times.

Resourcing Praise and Play

Your most important resource will be the adults who, in different ways, are involved in organizing, preparing for and leading the service. Try to build a team of leaders so that the various roles can be shared and responsibility does not fall on just one or two.

You will need people to lead the service. Your minister may like to be involved, but lay people could also lead. It is very helpful if the minister can be involved at least on some occasions, so that she or he can meet the group and they can meet her or him. You will also need other adults who are willing to 'support' —for example, those who will welcome people at the door, participate in the service and model what happens, prepare and set up the activities, or prepare and serve refreshments. Be cautious about involving adults whose children will be present in the service, as this can be difficult for both the adults and the children, and it may diminish the sense of a special time for the adult to share with their child.

In terms of equipment and materials, you do not need much to start with, but you should think about obtaining the following:

- A CD player and CDs (especially if you have no pianist or guitarist).
- Sturdy percussion instruments (such as the ones sold by The Early Learning Centre).
- Items for the focus table (see page 14 for more details).
- Basic craft materials (see page 19).
- Storytelling materials: if you are going to use the stories in this book, you will also need to gather together the necessary materials (see page 20).

Organizing Praise and Play

Because young children respond well to structure and routine, it is best to develop a pattern that you will follow each time. Here is one suggested pattern, but you may want to develop your own in ways that reflect something of the worship style of your own church.

- A time of gathering, which could include:
  - Building up a 'focus table'
  - A welcome song
  - Actions or rituals to help people move into a mood of worship
  - A gathering prayer
  - A song of praise

- The ministry of the word, which could include:
  - An activity to introduce the story
  - Telling the story
  - Finding the story in the Bible

- The response, which could include:
  - A conversation about the story
  - A song of praise or a song that relates to the story
  - A prayer arising out of the story
  - A craft activity

- The conclusion, which both brings the time of worship to a close and encourages people to look forward to going out. You might include:
  - A song
  - A blessing prayer
  - Actions or rituals to mark the ending of the worship

You may also want to include a time of sharing important items of news and celebrating birthdays or other significant events. After the structured time of worship, there can be a time for less structured activities and free play with toys, with drinks and a snack.

Unpacking Praise and Play

In this chapter, we shall consider particular elements from the *Praise and Play* service in greater detail.

Beginnings...

Corporate worship can be thought of as a kind of 'communal journey'. If you were to make a journey with a group of people, some of whom you had not seen for a while and others whom you may not have met before, you would probably take some time at the beginning to meet up, to get acquainted or reacquainted with each other, before turning your collective attention to the purpose for which you had gathered. Through words ('hello'; 'it's nice to see you'; 'welcome') and actions (shaking hands; a hug; a kiss), you would begin to form a community to make the journey together. Something similar can happen in worship: words and actions can be used to gather people together for the common purpose of worshipping God.

Here are some ideas to help you do this.

Building up the focus table

A table holding a display of appropriate objects gives a visual focus for the worship and helps to create a sense of being in a special and sacred place—a sense of purpose for the gathering.

Because young children are involved, it is important to give some thought to the height of the table: too high and they will not be able to see anything; too low and the objects will be too tempting for young children and can become a distraction rather than an attraction. If you are going to use a candle, you will certainly need to give careful attention to the height of the table and its position, in the interests of safety.

Think about what might be on the table. It could first be covered with a cloth. You could use a cloth that the group has helped to make, perhaps by sponge painting appropriate shapes on to plain coloured fabric, or you could have a series of cloths that relate to the natural seasons of the year (spring, summer, autumn, winter) or the church seasons (purple for Advent and Lent, white or gold for Christmas and Easter, and green for the times in between). Items to go on the table could include a cross, a candle, or a children's Bible. You could also include something that relates to the season, or the story to be told.

Setting up the table can become part of the gathering ritual. You could place all the items for the table in a special box and ask the group to help you unpack the box. Alternatively, you could hide the items at the back of the church and encourage the children and their carers to search them out. Young children love trying to find things that have been hidden and, having found them, they can bring them to the table at the front in procession (if a rather straggly one).

As far as possible, let members of the group set up the table themselves. It may not look as ordered as you would like it to be, but it is more important that the group should feel that they have contributed to it.

Singing a welcome song

You could welcome each other by engaging each person individually or by singing all together as a group. Think about how you can involve adults, too, so it does not become just a ritual for the children.

If the group is not too large, you could sing the following song to each individual child, to the tune of 'Frère Jacques' (adapted from the welcome song in *See and Know*: www.seeandknow.com).

Where is...? Where is...?
Did s/he come? Did s/he come?
Come to Praise and Play. *Come to* Praise and Play.
[Spoken] Is s/he here? [Shake hands with her/him.]

The following song could be sung by a larger group in two halves.

Welcome, welcome.
Welcome, welcome.
We're glad that you have come;
We're glad that you have come.
Welcome, welcome.
Welcome, welcome
From each and every one.
From each and every one.

Welcome, welcome.
Welcome, welcome.
We're glad that you belong;
We're glad that you belong;
Welcome, welcome.
Welcome, welcome.
From each and every one.
From each and every one.

FROM *COME AND PRAISE BEGINNING* SONG BOOK, PAGE 26, OR CD 1, TRACK 11.

Praying a gathering prayer

A gathering prayer is a short prayer asking God to come close to the group in the worship. An example of a gathering prayer might be:

Dear God, be with us in our 'Praise and Play'. Help us to have a special time with you and a special time with each other. Amen

Actions and rituals

Light a candle, encouraging a mood of quiet and a sense of awe as you do so. You may want to accompany the action with some words that are repeated each week. An example might be:

We light the 'Praise and Play' candle to help us remember that we have come to spend a special time with God and a special time with each other.

Ring a bell while the children sing a song. You may also want to accompany the ringing with some words that are repeated each week. An example might be:

Ring, ring, ring the bell,
We're glad that we are here;
Ring, ring, ring the bell,
We know that God is near.
SUNG TO THE TUNE OF 'ROW, ROW, ROW THE BOAT'

... and endings

Just as you might develop a pattern of words, actions and rituals for gathering people together at the beginning of the worship, so it is important to develop a pattern for the way you finish. Here are some ideas.

Praying a blessing prayer

A blessing prayer may be spoken or sung. Examples might include a blessing with the group divided into two halves, such as the one below.

The love of God
The love of God
Be with us
Be with us
For ever more,
For ever more,
Amen
Amen
FROM *COME AND PRAISE BEGINNING* SONG BOOK, PAGE 48

Alternatively, you may choose to use a circle blessing, such as the one below. Stand in a circle holding hands, looking to left and right at the appropriate words.

God bless you who are on my left,
And God bless you on my right;
May God keep you safe all through the day
And guard you all through the night.
FROM *A LITTLE BOOK OF BLESSINGS*, ED. SOPHIE PIPER (LIONHUDSON)

Actions and rituals

If you have lit a candle at the beginning of your service, you need to extinguish it at the end. This can be done in a number of ways. If your group is fairly small, all could gather around and blow on the count of three. If you have a larger group, someone whose birthday or special day it is could blow out the candle, or you could develop a system of turn-taking. An alternative to blowing is to use a candle snuffer—and then watch the smoke go up into the air.

Together, pack away the items from the 'focus table' in their own box. This is a way of showing that the items for the table are special and, at a practical level, it keeps them together and in good condition.

Music and singing

Many young children love singing, and you don't need to feel that you have to be an expert. Here are some suggestions to bear in mind.

- Choose short songs and sing them several times, particularly when you introduce a new song. Young children love repetition and it helps them to remember the songs. Songs that have 'built in' repetition of words and lines are particularly easy to learn.
- Choose songs that have a straightforward tune with an easily recognized rhythm.
- Build up a repertoire of favourites, and don't introduce too many at once.
- If you have no pianist or guitarist, use worship CDs and sing along to them.
- Let the children choose the songs sometimes.
- You might want to include some secular songs or rhymes that fit a particular theme.

Try accompanying a song with:

- simple percussion instruments
- finger play
- actions
- holding items linked with the song
- actions around a circle of two-way stretch lycra, used like a mini-parachute

Some ideas to try might include the following:

- Give out soft toy sheep so that each child can hold one as you sing a song about sheep and shepherds—for example, 'The Lord, the Lord' (*Come and Praise Beginning*, CD 1, track 16).
- Invite the group to sit around a circle of two-way stretch lycra as you sing 'Jesus' love is very wonderful' (*Come and Praise Beginning* songbook page 70. A CD version is on *God's Wonderful World*, track 14). Hold the fabric around the edge, making gentle waves as you sing the verse; when you sing the chorus, lift the fabric high (for 'so high you can't get over it'), then low (for 'so low you can't get under it') and then stretch it out (for 'so wide you can't get round it').
- Give out simple percussion instruments to use with a song such as 'What noise shall we make to say that God is great?' (CD: *God's Wonderful World*, track 1).
- Make up actions to go with 'When I get up in the morning' (CD: *I Know Jesus Loves Me* with Ishmael).
- Use a song to pray, such as 'Thank you, Lord, for this fine day'. Encourage the children to give their

suggestions of things they would like to thank God for, although you may have to work their ideas into the rhythm of the song.

Useful music resources might include:

- *God's Wonderful World* and *Thank You, God, for Snails*, Julia Plaut (Kingsway Music)
- *Come and Praise Beginning*, Song book and two CDs (BBC Education)
- *I Know Jesus Loves Me*, Ishmael (Children's Ministry)

The ministry of the word (the story)

As with any other form of worship, the Bible (God's story) plays a significant part in *Praise and Play*. Young children love stories and we can tell stories to them in all kinds of ways. In this book, a particular approach to storytelling is used—one that resembles the way young children themselves often tell stories in their own play. It draws on the idea of 'playmats' or 'builder's trays' that depict particular scenes with which young children are very familiar. The stories are played out on appropriately coloured pieces of fabric—for example, sand for the wilderness, green for grass, blue for water and so on. Wooden bricks are used to make the bases of buildings, and small-scale figures are used for people, animals and objects. (See page 20 for more detailed notes on making the story materials.) In this way, the stories are told not just with words but also visually, with movement, and young children are engaged far more effectively. Pre-school children make more sense of situations intuitively from what they see and experience than from spoken language; using this approach, they become more engaged, more excited and more intrigued by the biblical stories.

The sessions in this book are built around stories about Jesus or told by him. Jesus, of course, is central to our Christian faith, but telling young children about him is not as easy as is sometimes supposed. Too often, when we tell young children about Jesus, we are in danger of presenting him in a rather straightforward way, as 'a good man' who cared for people, made those who were unwell better and told stories about how people can live better lives. But Jesus is more than 'a good man' and these are more than straightforward stories. At one level, each story relates to things that were of a particular time and place. At other levels, however, each one also opens up windows on to the kingdom of God, where all are welcome (see 'The man with a hundred sheep', page 44), where there is no more sickness (see 'Jesus heals an older woman and a young girl', page 40), where there is no more fear (see 'Jesus calms a storm', page 47), where everyone lives with God's abundant overflowing generosity (see 'Jesus feeds a great crowd', page 50) and where suffering is transformed into new life (see 'Jesus appears to Mary Magdalene', page 56).

These stories are intended to lead us to recognition of and faith in Jesus as the incarnate Son of God. Towards the end of his Gospel, John wrote, 'These are written so that you will put your faith in Jesus as the Messiah and the Son of God. If you have faith in him, you will have true life' (John 20:31). Part of our task in telling young children the stories is to introduce them to Jesus in ways that will open up their hearts and minds to *something* of this faith, and you will see that the introduction to each of the stories in this book sets the scene for an understanding that it is about more than just 'a good man'. Of course, this assumes that we are looking through a long-term lens, so the way in which we tell the stories even to very young children is important not just for the present but also for the way they might engage with biblical stories and with the person of Jesus in the future, and how they might be enabled to make deeper and more enlarged meanings from the stories as they get older.

The principle adopted in this book is not to present 'young children's stories' (children grow out of 'young children's stories') but to present stories that young children can engage with and from which they can gain some meaning. Clearly, the authors of biblical stories did not have children in mind as they wrote, and we need to be alert to important ideas or vocabulary in the Bible that might be alien to, or too complex for, young children and might need some alteration or explanation. Nor does the approach to storytelling adopted here try to impose adult understandings on the children's experience of the story. Rather, it offers children space to encounter the story and make sense of it as they are able, with all the experience, knowledge, skills and sensitivities that they possess as 2–4 year olds. As they encounter each story in the *Praise and Play* service, they will not understand everything about it (nor do you or I!) but that means there is more to be discovered the next time they meet the story.

Although the storytelling part of this book was developed very much with young children in mind, its approach has proved to engage adults as well, both those who have little experience of the Bible and those who are familiar with it.

No single telling of a biblical story can say everything there is to say about that story, so we need to be constantly open to the possibility that God will reveal new insights and connections each time we encounter a story—and that is true for the storyteller as well as for those who are listening. If we are telling very familiar stories to young children, it is all too easy to rely on our memory of the narrative as we have encountered it thus far. But it is important for the teller to spend time with the story before the *Praise and Play* service, not just practising how to communicate it, but also reflecting personally and prayerfully on it. We cannot, with integrity, expect children or adults to be excited about biblical stories if we are not still being 'lit up' by them. Therefore, there are some short notes for the storyteller at the beginning of each session, offering some additional thoughts, which, in turn, might lead into new insights and more enlarged meanings of the passage. Bible commentaries also help us to enlarge our understanding of biblical material and BRF's *People's Bible Commentary* series is recommended. (For individual titles and further information, see www.brf.org.uk.)

Setting up the story

The stories in the Bible are, in many ways, removed from young children's experience, so children need help to get into the situation of the story. Setting up the story with the children is a vital preliminary activity and really helps them to engage with it. It is suggested that all the materials for a particular story are placed in a story basket before the *Praise and Play* service begins. A picnic basket with a lid serves this purpose well. You need just one basket, because you can change the materials each week to tell a different story.

As you bring out the same story basket each time, at the appropriate moment in the service, the group will recognize it and know what is going to happen next. As you open the basket and begin to take out the items, you will immediately capture the group's attention and sense of wonder. In each session plan, there is a suggested outline for the way in which you could set the story up and the conversations you might have with the children as you do so. Practise the outline a few times on your own, but do not feel that you have to follow it word for word: the important thing is to prepare the group to encounter the story by creating a mood of excitement and anticipation that draws people into the story as you begin to tell it.

You can also develop a pattern for setting up the storytelling space. Encourage people to sit in a circle around the space: they may want to sit on cushions or kneelers.

Telling the story

Although there is a script and choreography (instructions on how to use the story materials) for each story in the session outlines, storytelling is best done without reference to a script or notes. This can seem very daunting, especially if you are new to storytelling, so here is a step-by-step guide to help you in your preparation.

- First, spend time with the biblical story yourself. Prayerfully, read and reflect on the story from the Bible itself, and allow it to become a part of you. It may be helpful to imagine the story in your mind, or sketch it out in a series of frames. To do this, fold a piece of A4 paper into six or eight sections and draw a simple picture in each section (stick people are fine!) to help you remember the key parts of the story and the order in which events occur.
- Then read through the story and the movements as developed in the session outline. Do not try to remember the whole story word for word; story-telling is as much the work of the heart and spirit as of the memory.
- Next, gather all the storytelling materials together.
- Practise telling the story with the materials, and with the book open to one side. You will need to do this several times, but each time try to rely less and less on the book. There may be some parts of the story that you do want to express in a precise way, and it is helpful to identify them, but remember that you are not trying to learn the whole story by heart.
- Then try telling the story without the book. Again, you will need to do this a few times. Practise speaking in a calm and measured way. At this stage, do not allow yourself to look at the book until you have told the whole story. In this way you will learn to let your heart for the story take over. You will also find that the materials offer you cues if your mind goes completely blank.

When you are with the group:

- Tell the story in a calm and measured way. The stories may seem very demanding of young children's concentration span, but you will be surprised at how engaged they become.
- Arrange with other helpers beforehand that they should try to respond to any 'disruptions' to the story so that the storyteller does not need to break off to deal with anything else.
- Discourage the children from interrupting or touching the story materials while you are telling the story, unless, of course, you have specifically asked

them to do something. Explain that they can have their turn later to play with the story.
- When you are ready to put the story away, let the children help you (they will anyway!) and if you direct the 'putting away' it will be done in a more ordered way.

Responding to the story

Any conversations about the story may be fairly short because young children have limited language skills and their prime concern is with what they want to say themselves. But the group can be encouraged to talk about which parts of the story they liked and which they did not like. Young children also enjoy placing 'themselves' in the story. Try to have a basket of spare figures so that each child can do this in a very 'concrete' way. Encourage the adults to lay down a figure for themselves, but not to influence the children in how they place theirs. There are no right answers in these kinds of conversations, but it is one way in which we can help children to engage with biblical stories with their hearts and spirits as well as with their minds.

At the end of the telling, it can be helpful to find the story in the Bible on the focus table. You could make a special bookmark and put it in place before the start of *Praise and Play*.

Praying with young children

In each session outline, there is a suggestion for a simple prayer that makes a connection between a theme from the story and the children's own experience. It invites some contribution from the group, which you can include when you pray the prayer.

Activities

Included in each session outline is an idea for a pre-prepared individual activity and a collective activity. The materials required are readily available in most craft shops. Encourage carers to work with their children: this is an opportunity for them to do the activities together, and, because of the age of the children, adult help is invaluable. It is also helpful to produce a 'here's one I made earlier' sample so that everyone can see what they are aiming for.

Message labels

With the individual activities, there is a message label to be attached to each activity. Children will not usually be able to read the message for themselves, but it reminds the carers of the story so that they can recall it with their children later, and it also provides a conversation cue for the parent(s) who were not present, when the children get home. The easiest way to produce the message is on the computer, where you only need to type it out once and then copy it in repeated text boxes.

Pictures

Some of the activities require pictures, which you can gather from a number of sources. Magazines and supplements are a good source of pictures of people and food. Gardening catalogues give an abundance of small pictures of flowers, plants, fruit and vegetables. You can also use electronic sources such as photocopiable clip art or downloadable images found on the Internet using a search engine such as Google Images.

Open activities

In addition to the pre-prepared activities, try to have some materials available for one or two more open activities so that children (and adults, if they wish) can create their own work in response to the story. This can be particularly useful for older children in the group who may want to spend more time doing activities.

The materials can be varied from week to week and might include:

- Ready mixed paints and brushes or small square sponges
- Playdough and appropriate tools
- Collage materials
- Junk modelling
- Construction sets

You could also set out some toys, jigsaws and books, appropriate for the age range of the children. In addition, you may be able to set up some play activities that relate to the story.

NB: Check the toys regularly to make sure that they are clean, safe and complete.

Food for snack time

Some of the food ideas lend themselves to involvement with the children, but this will depend on your facilities. In some cases, it may be more practical for the food to be pre-prepared by the *Praise and Play* team.

NB: Be aware of food allergies, such as wheat, milk and nut allergies. Parents and carers should advise you of any problems in this respect so that certain foods can be avoided or alternatives offered as appropriate.

Storytelling materials

Below is a list of the materials that you will need to tell the stories in this book. There are some basic items, which are used in several stories, but the other items are specific to particular stories.

Basic items

First of all, you will need a story basket—a picnic basket with a hinged lid makes a good one. You will also need a selection of smaller bowl-shaped wicker baskets, which will fit inside the story basket to hold groups of items, making them easier to find.

Fabric items

- A sand-coloured story cloth, approx. 120cm x 100cm.
- A piece of green fabric for a grassy area, approx. 50cm x 40cm (with a wavy line cut along the edges).
- A piece of blue fabric for water, approx. 90cm x 70 cm (with a wavy line cut along the edges).
- A piece of brown or grey fabric for a roadway, approx. 120cm x 15cm.

The fabric for these pieces could be felt (which is not washable) or fleece (which is washable). It is important that the fabric should be durable and should not fray.

Wooden items

- Wooden bricks, which will be used to make the bases for buildings.
- A boat, approx. 30cm x 8cm. This should be a simple boat shape, hollowed out in the middle so that the disciples can be placed in it. If you are unable to make a wooden boat, try to find a suitable toy one (preferably wooden).
- A table, approx. 18cm x 7cm.
- Animal figures: six sheep and one wolf. If you cannot buy or make wooden figures, you could use animals from farm sets.
- People figures, in at least two sizes to represent children and adults. You will need 15–20 adult figures and about six child figures. The figures used

to trial the materials in this book were a basic cone shape with a sphere on the top, and are part of a range called 'Lara's Wood Shapes', made by Lara's Crafts. (This is an American company but does supply craft shops in the UK. You could also try Internet shopping.) The adult figures are 9cm high, and the child figures are 5cm high.

It is helpful to paint the 'bodies' in different colours to help children identify the characters in the story, but do not add in any other features. Most of the figures can assume different characters in different stories, but you will need some specific figures, such as:

- The 'earthly' Jesus, painted brown with a purple sash over one shoulder.
- The resurrected Jesus, painted white with the same sash over one shoulder, signifying that, although the resurrected Jesus had changed, some things about him were recognizable.
- Four angels, painted white with a gold band around the neck.
- A small wooden figure for the baby Jesus.

If possible, try to have a special set of figures that are kept especially for telling these stories. An alternative to the wooden figures described above would be spun paper finger puppets, which are the same shape and can be purchased from www.tts-group.co.uk or www.mjjeducation.com. They come in packs of 30, in three different heights. As these figures are only available in white, it is suggested that you paint them a pale fawn first.

NB: Whether you are painting wooden or paper figures, make sure you use paint that conforms to child safety standards and is lead-free.

You may also wish to have additional figures so that the group can place themselves in the story during the conversations afterwards.

Specific items

The additional items, needed for particular stories, are listed below. They can be obtained from craft suppliers, or some of them could be made.

Session 1

- A manger and some straw
- A strip of white cloth

Session 2

- A gold star, about 4cm long, made from wood or card
- Three small boxes wrapped up as presents
- A gold crown to fit on one of the figures, made from card

Session 3

- A net, made from a fruit or vegetable net
- Some fish, made from wood or Fimo

Session 6

- A small padded 'mattress' or rug

Session 7

- Some coloured felt shapes (see page 45 for details)

Session 9

- Five loaves made from Fimo
- Two fish made from Fimo or wood
- Two small plates
- Twelve small baskets
- Some small pieces of green fabric, to simulate patches of grass

Session 10

- A tree, made from wood or stout card

Session 11

- A tomb, made from modroc or by arranging some large stones. Make the tomb with a wide entrance so that you will be able to stand two angel figures in it.
- A large stone
- A free-standing cross, about 16cm high

NB: modroc is like a roll of bandage, but it is covered with plaster of paris. Before using the modroc, make an outline shape for the tomb with chicken wire. Cut off pieces of modroc and wet them. Lay them over the wire frame and leave to dry. Once dry, the tomb can be painted with craft paint.

Session 12

- A free-standing cross (as in Session 11)
- A cloud shape cut from a piece of white felt

NB: Because of the small items, children should be supervised at all times when they have access to these story materials.

Jesus is born

Bible reference: Luke 2:1–20

This must be the best-known story of Jesus for young children. Many 'early years' groups, even those that are not connected with a church, will, through story and drama, rhyme and music, tell the story of Jesus' birth: the long journey to Bethlehem with Mary riding a donkey, the frustrating attempts to find a room in the overcrowded hotels, the offer of a stable with animals lying peacefully around on sweet-smelling hay, and the birth of the baby Jesus who rests in the manger while Mary sits serenely nearby and Joseph stands protectively over them both. But look again at the passage in Luke's Gospel, and you will see that imaginative embellishments have become embedded into the core of the story. So what has been added in?

Let's explore further...

In Luke's account there is no mention of a donkey—although it is not unreasonable to imagine Mary riding on a donkey, as the journey between Nazareth and Bethlehem was about 110km (70 miles) and donkeys were the most common form of transport. Nor is there any specific mention of a 'stable', and that tradition may have emerged by deduction from the reference to Jesus being placed in an animal's feeding trough (or manger). It's also quite likely that the word translated as 'inn' does not correspond to 'hotel' as we know it. It is possible that part of Joseph's extended family already lived in Bethlehem, and Luke may have been describing the kind of house that had two floors, in which the ground floor was usually kept for animals while people lived and slept upstairs. There may even have been a guest area. Perhaps Mary and Joseph had to stay on the ground floor, because the guest area upstairs was already too crowded. Although this floor would have had the trappings associated with animals (hence the manger), there is no suggestion that animals were actually present.

It is tempting to overlook the significance in the story of the strips of cloth and the manger (v. 12). Our carefully crafted nativity scenes depict the stable as an isolated and 'obvious' building for the shepherds to find, but, if Mary and Joseph were staying in a house, it would have been one among many and there may have been other newborn babies in Bethlehem that night. The shepherds could have been in for a long search. The strips of cloth and the manger were signs given by the angel so that the shepherds would know that *this* was the baby they were looking for.

The shepherds are significant in Luke's account for a number of reasons. They represent society's poor and marginalized, who, along with the lame, the blind and the oppressed, feature so strongly in Luke's Gospel as rightfully belonging to the kingdom of God. But more than this, there had been a long tradition of 'shepherding' as an image for leadership of the Jewish people. The prophet Ezekiel had criticized the leaders of his day and prophesied that, one day, God would come as a very different kind of shepherd (Ezekiel 34). Here, then, we see the shepherds from the fields paying homage to the baby who would grow up to be *the* Shepherd.

The part of Luke's passage that is often omitted in retellings for children is the response of the shepherds after they had found the baby. They didn't keep this discovery to themselves but made known not just the existence of the baby but 'what the angel had said about him' (v. 17), and they returned to their sheep 'glorifying and praising God for all they had heard and seen' (v. 20, NRSV).

So can it be said that the story of Jesus' birth is a story for young children? Yes, of course, but the challenge is to generate among the children, and the adults with them, something of the wonder that the shepherds first experienced, so that they too want to respond by 'praising and glorifying God'. Luke tells us an amazing story! The birth of any baby is special, but he is not telling us of the birth of any baby, but the birth of the one who is 'a Saviour… Christ the Lord' (v. 11).

He is telling of the incarnation: in this baby, born of a single mother in a place usually kept for animals, whose only visitors on that first night were some lowly shepherds—in this baby God became human. Does this make your heart leap? Does it make you say 'Wow'? The danger is that we can romanticize and embellish the story so much that the true focus of it is lost.

 ## The story

See notes on storytelling materials on page 20.

You will need:

* The story basket
* The sand-coloured story cloth
* Fabric for the road
* Green fabric for the fields
* Wooden bricks in a basket, enough to make the base of a house
* A manger and straw
* Figures: Mary, Joseph, baby, four angels, three shepherds, some sheep (Group the figures in smaller baskets)
* A strip of white cloth

Setting up the story

(Bring out the story basket and create an air of mystery as you open it.) I wonder who or what our story is going to be about today?

I wonder where our story will be? *(Lay out the sand-coloured story cloth.)*

How might you get from there *(point to the right-hand edge of the story cloth)* to there *(move your hand across to the other side of the story cloth)*, or from there to there? *(Reverse movement. Talk about the possibilities.)*

We need a road! *(Bring out the strip of fabric for the road, and lay it across the story cloth.)*

Maybe it's not all sand and road. I've got something else here. *(Hold out the green fabric before laying it down on the far left of the cloth.)* What might this be?

Do you think anything or anyone stays here? Let's see if there's anything else in the story basket. Yes, there are some sheep. *(Bring out the sheep and place them on the grass.)*

Will the sheep be all right by themselves or do they need someone to look after them? *(Allow time for the children to make their own suggestions and then look in the story basket.)*

Let's see, yes—some people to look after the sheep. We call them shepherds. *(Place three shepherds with the sheep.)*

There's something else—a basket of bricks. *(Bring out the basket of bricks and start to play with them.)* What might these be in the story? *(Gradually build a base for the house to the left of the middle of the story cloth, next to and on your side of the road.)*

It could be a house, but there's something to go in this place. *(Bring out the manger.)* It's got straw in it… it's a feeding box for animals—sometimes it's called a manger—so maybe some animals sometimes live here. I wonder if people could live here, too? I wonder what it would be like to stay in here?

(Sit back and view the story cloth.)

So… a road, a kind of house with a manger in it, some fields with some sheep and some shepherds. *(Touch or point to the different parts as you remind children of the features.)* I think we've got everything we need to start. Are you ready for our story?

Telling the story

The people living in this place *(move hand across the story cloth)* were very unhappy, but God had promised them that—when the time was right—he would send a special person to rescue them, to make them happy and safe and more like how God wanted them to be. But who would this special person be? *(Pause before continuing the story.)*

Once there was a woman called Mary. *(Hold Mary in the palm of your hand.)* She was having a baby. An angel had told Mary that the baby she was carrying was very special; her baby was the Son of God.

Mary lived in a house in Nazareth. *(Place Mary by the road at the far right-hand side.)* She was engaged to a man called Joseph. *(Take out Joseph and hold him in the palm of your hand.)* Joseph took good care of Mary. *(Place Joseph next to Mary.)*

One day, Mary and Joseph had to make a long

journey to a town called Bethlehem… *(move your hand over the left part of the story cloth, then begin to move the figures along the road)* the town where the great king David had once lived.

It was a long way from Nazareth to Bethlehem, and it was a hard journey, especially for Mary because she was having the baby.

After many days travelling, they got to Bethlehem. *(Rest the figures on the road, before the stable.)* Lots and lots of people were there, all needing a place to stay. And do you know where Mary and Joseph had to stay? They had to stay in a place where animals sometimes lived. *(Move the figures into the 'stable'.)*

While they were there, the time came for Mary to have her baby. She gave birth to her firstborn son *(place the baby Jesus in your hands)*, she wrapped him in strips of cloth *(wrap strip of white cloth around the baby)* and she put him in an animals' feeding box. *(Bring out the baby and lay him in the feeding box.)* And there the baby lay.

It was night time and, out on the hills, the shepherds were looking after their sheep. *(Indicate the shepherds and sheep by circling your left hand over that part of the story cloth.)* Now we would think that looking after sheep was a very important job but, in this place, people didn't think shepherds were very important at all.

When these very ordinary shepherds looked up, standing before them was an angel from God… *(place angel figure near the shepherds)* and there was bright light shining all around. The shepherds were really frightened.

But the angel said, 'Don't be frightened. I am bringing you good news that is going to bring great joy to everyone. Today God's special person has been born in Bethlehem. You will find him as a baby wrapped in strips of cloth and lying in an animal's feeding box.'

Suddenly, there were lots of angels *(place other three angels around the first angel)*, all praising God and saying, 'Praise God in heaven!'

Then the angels went away. *(Take the angels away.)* The shepherds raced to find God's special person, the baby whom the angel had told them about. *(Move the shepherds along the road towards the 'stable'.)* They found the baby, just as the angel had said, wrapped in strips of cloth and lying in the animals' feeding box… *(arrange the shepherds around the manger)* with Mary and Joseph close by.

When they left, the shepherds told other people about the baby and what the angel had said. *(Scatter the shepherds to different parts of the story cloth.)* Then, as they returned to the fields, they thanked God for all that they had seen and heard. *(Move the shepherds back to the fields.)*

(Take the baby and hold it in the palm of your hand.) This is God's special person. He will be like a light from heaven, shining on all who are sad or frightened or want to be better people.

Talking about the story

✪ Talk about which part of the story the children liked best.
✪ Was there anything they did not like?
✪ Where would they like to be in the story? (If possible, have a basket of spare figures so that they can put themselves in the story.)
✪ Who is God's special person?

Prayer

Christmas is a happy time for many people, but some people are sad. Ask if anyone knows someone who will be sad this Christmas.

Dear God, you came to earth in Jesus so that you could be close to people, especially people who are sad. Please be close to everyone who is sad at Christmas time, especially… Amen

Individual craft activity

Nativity plaques

For each child you will need:
✳ A paper plate with a hole punched at the top
✳ Strips of orange, yellow and red tissue paper
✳ Simple line drawings of Mary, Joseph and the manger and baby (see template, page 64)
✳ Message label saying: The angel said to the shepherds, 'Don't be frightened! God's special person has been born today.' (Luke 2:10, adapted)
✳ A length of wool or ribbon for a hanging thread
✳ Watered-down PVA glue and a glue spreader

Spread glue over the plate and cover completely with the strips of coloured tissue paper. (Adult task: trim around the edge of the plate to remove any overhanging bits of tissue paper.) When the plate is covered, spread a thin layer of glue over the tissue paper. Place the cut-out line drawings in the middle of the plaque. Attach the message label at the bottom and thread the hanging thread through the hole in the top.

Group craft activity

Greetings wreath

Make a greetings wreath to give to a group in the community, such as those living at a local residential home.

You will need:
* White card
* Green sugar paper
* A nativity picture
* PVA glue
* Red finger paint
* Red crêpe paper
* Card to make a message label

Cut out a large circle of card. The size of the circle will depend on the number of people in your group. Draw a smaller circle in the middle and stick on a nativity picture. You could use an old Christmas card or download a picture from the Internet.

Draw around everyone's hands using green sugar paper and cut out the shapes. Stick them outside the small circle, with the fingers towards the outer edge. Curling the fingers gives added effect. Using red finger paint, invite everyone to add some 'berries'.

Make a big red bow from crêpe paper and stick it at the bottom of the wreath.

Make a message label saying 'A happy Christmas to everyone' and attach it to the middle of the bow.

Snack time

Decorate Christmas biscuits

Make a basic biscuit dough using your own recipe or the one below.

You will need:
300g self-raising flour; 200g butter or margarine; 200g caster sugar; 1 egg (beaten); icing sugar and a selection of cake decorations; mixing spoon or hand-held mixer; small rolling pins; Christmas pastry cutters; baking parchment or greaseproof paper dusted with flour; baking tray.

Put the flour into a bowl. Rub in the butter or margarine, then stir in the sugar. Mix to a stiff dough with the beaten egg. Knead lightly until smooth.

The dough should be rolled out to about 5mm thickness and then cut out with Christmas cutters, such as stars or angels. Decorate the biscuits with icing and other cake decorations.

Place each biscuit on a square of baking parchment, marked with the child's name, then put the biscuits on a baking tray and bake them. If you have no kitchen facilities, the children could take their biscuits home unbaked, with instructions on how to bake them at home. The biscuits will need to be baked in an oven pre-heated to Gas Mark 3/325°F/170°C for about 18 minutes.

NB: Make sure the children wash their hands before the activity. If you have no water connection, have available a plastic washing-up bowl, water warmed in a kettle, some soap and towels. As with any food activity, check whether any child has allergies, and, as the biscuit recipe has egg in it, make sure the children don't eat the raw dough.

The wise men visit Jesus

Bible reference: Matthew 2:1–12

The story of the wise men frequently features as part of the pre-Christmas nativity stories and dramas, when there is a great temptation to pick out only the 'cosy' bits of the story and add the characters in as just another set of visitors to the baby Jesus. However, this story really belongs to the period of time after Christmas and is remembered at the feast of the Epiphany (which means *showing*) on 6 January. If we read the whole story, we discover that it is far from 'cosy'.

Let's explore further...

Although the wise men are sometimes referred to (or portrayed) as kings, it is more accurate to call them wise men or magi. They were wealthy and learned men, particularly knowledgeable about astronomy. The biblical narrative does not say how many magi visited, only that there were three gifts. They came from the east, and would have been Gentiles—that is, not of the Jewish faith.

Kings and kingship are themes that run strongly through this story, however. The wise men have identified the change in the stars as heralding the birth of a child 'born to be king of the Jews' (v. 2), so they go first to the existing king of the Jews to ask where the new king of the Jews has been born. Maybe they are not so wise after all! Nevertheless, their misguided action highlights some marked contrasts between the existing king of the Jews and the one born to be *the* king of the Jews. One lives in a publicly recognizable palace in the great city of Jerusalem, the other in a house in Bethlehem, so obscure that it needs the star to point the way; one has a power built on cruelty, the other a

power built on love; one has a self-centred authority, the other a God-centred authority; one is an adult, the other a vulnerable baby.

Threatened by what the wise men say, the existing 'king of the Jews' immediately plots against the new 'king of the Jews'. He first tries to trick the wise men, and when that fails, he orders the killing of all the children under the age of two in and around Bethlehem—reminiscent of the order that Pharaoh gave centuries before (Exodus 1:22), when he felt threatened by the Hebrew slaves living in Egypt. But just as Moses was saved from Pharaoh's cruelty, so Jesus will be saved from Herod's cruelty.

What seemingly strange gifts to bring a baby! Different ideas exist about the significance of the gifts. Some people believe that the gold is symbolic of kingship, the frankincense of priesthood and the myrrh of Jesus' death. Others think that all three might just have been gifts fit for a king. Whatever their significance, there must have been something rather incongruous about leaving those expensive and rarefied gifts with a seemingly ordinary family in an out-of-the-way house in Bethlehem.

So can it be said that this is a passage for young children? Yes, but it is an account that stands in its own right and, as such, shouldn't just be tacked on to the pre-Christmas nativity story. We should also tell something of the uncomfortable bits of the story, even to young children.

The story

See notes on storytelling materials on page 20.

You will need:
* The story basket
* The sand-coloured story cloth
* The fabric for the road
* A basket of wooden bricks
* A gold star, about 4cm, made of wood or card
* Three small boxes wrapped to look like presents
* Figures of Mary, Joseph, baby Jesus, Herod (with a gold crown made from card), and three or four wise men

Setting up the story

(Bring out the story basket and create an air of mystery as you open it.) I wonder who or what our story is going to be about today? I wonder where our story will be? *(Lay out the sand-coloured story cloth.)*

How might you get from there *(point to the right hand edge of the story cloth)* to there… *(move your hand across to the other side of the story cloth)*, or from there to there? *(Reverse movement. Talk about the possibilities.)*

We need a road! *(Bring out the strip of fabric for the road, and lay it across the story cloth.)*

(Bring out the basket of bricks.) What might these be in the story? *(Build the base of Joseph and Mary's house on the left side of the story cloth, with the entrance on to the road.)*

Who might live here? *(Bring out Mary, Joseph and Jesus.)* I wonder who they might be? *(The children may tell you themselves, but establish the characters' names before moving on.)*

(Bring out Herod.) This place was ruled by a king. This king is called King Herod. *(Place Herod near the road on your right and then sit back and view the story cloth.)*

So… a road, a house for Joseph and Mary and Jesus, and a king. *(Touch or point to the different parts as you remind children of the features.)* I think we've got everything we need to start. Are you ready for our story?

Telling the story

The people living in this place *(move hand across the story cloth)* were very unhappy, but God had promised them that—when the time was right—he would send a special person to rescue them, a new kind of king, to make them happy and safe and more like how God wanted them to be. But who would this special person be? *(Pause before continuing the story.)*

There were some people, some wise men, who knew a lot about the stars in the sky. *(Bring out the wise men and place them on the right-hand edge of the road.)* They had seen a new star in the sky *(hold the star on the palm of your hand)* and they thought this star was a sign that a special new king had been born. *(Hold the star in your left hand above the road on the story cloth.)* The star moved in the sky and the wise men followed it. *(Move the star ahead of the wise men with your left hand, as you move the wise men one at a time with your right hand towards Herod.)*

The wise men went to King Herod. *(Stand the wise men in front of Herod, and lay the star down by your side. Move Herod nearer the wise men. Shake your head as you say…)* But the new king wasn't there. King Herod didn't know anything about a new king.

Now some kings in the Bible are good kings and they care about people, but some kings are bad kings and they don't care about people; they only care about themselves. King Herod was a bad king and he only cared about himself. He didn't want there to be another king—he was the king. He said *(raise your forefinger as if giving a command)*, 'Go and find the child who is this new special king, and then tell me where he is, so I too can go and see him.' But King Herod was trying to trick the wise men.

The wise men followed the star again until it stopped over the house where the child Jesus was. *(Pick up the star and move it from Herod to the house with your left hand. Move the wise men, one at a time, with your right hand. Lay the star down by your side.)*

They were full of joy and went into the house. *(Move the wise men into the house.)* There they saw the child Jesus with Mary his mother, and they

Reproduced with permission from *Praise and Play!* published by BRF 2009 (978 1 84101 563 7) www.barnabasinchurches.org.uk

27

knelt down. They opened their treasure chests and gave him the gifts they had brought—gold and frankincense and myrrh. *(Take out the three presents from the story basket and place them by Jesus.)*

Then the wise men had a dream, which warned them not to go back to Herod, so they left and went a different way home. *(Move the wise men along the road, towards the left-hand edge of the story cloth, and then return them to the basket.)*

Talking about the story

- ✪ Talk about which part of the story the children liked best.
- ✪ Was there anything they did not like?
- ✪ Where would they like to be in the story? (If possible, have a basket of spare figures so that they can put themselves in the story.)

Prayer

The wise men were full of joy when they found Jesus. Talk about what makes us full of joy.

Dear Jesus, thank you for… because they make us feel full of joy. Amen

Individual craft activity

A present for the family

For each child, you will need:

- ✳ A plain envelope, approx. 23cm x 16cm. Stick down the flap, then cut away two adjacent corners from a short side (see diagram). If you open out the envelope, you will see that you have a gift bag, the handle being the edge between the two cutaway corners
- ✳ Paper shapes to decorate
- ✳ Enough wrapped sweets or chocolates to provide one for each member of the family
- ✳ A label saying 'With love from…'
- ✳ Glue sticks and crayons (for the group as a whole)

Write the child's name on the label. Encourage children to do this themselves if they can. Glue the message on to the middle of one side of the gift bag. Decorate the

bag by sticking shapes on both sides. Count out enough wrapped sweets or chocolates for each member of the child's family and put them in the gift bag. Explain that this is a present for them to give to their family. Assure them that there is a sweet for everyone, including them, but that they should try to share the present all together.

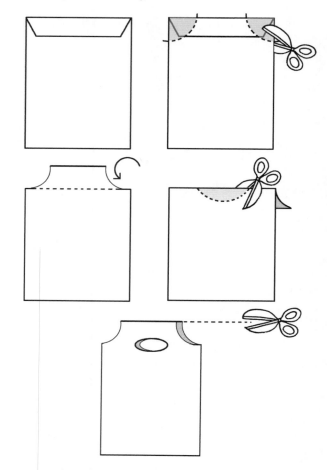

Group craft activity

Star garland

Make a star garland to hang. Pre-cut large stars from card (see template on page 65). Punch a hole near the tip of one point on each star. In the group, decorate the stars with collage materials. Thread hanging threads through the holes. Hang the stars from a string stretched across the room.

Snack time

Make star shaped biscuits, which the children could decorate. You can find a recipe on page 30 of *Christmas Make and Do* (see Bibliography, page 74).

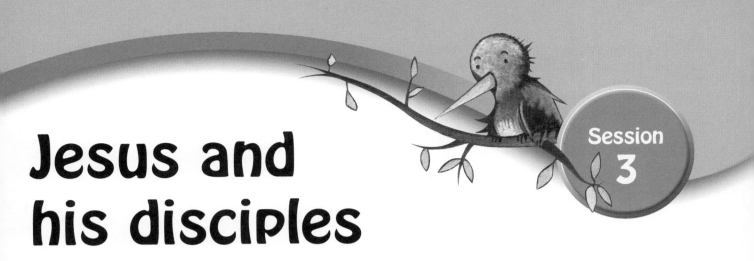

Jesus and his disciples

Bible reference: Luke 5:1–11

This passage has much in common with a 'miraculous catch' story in John's Gospel, although the context of John's account is after the resurrection (John 21:1–23). In Luke's Gospel, the miracle takes place near the beginning of Jesus' ministry, but we see that enough time has passed for Jesus to be well known, because 'the people… crowded around him to hear God's message' (v. 1). We also know that Jesus and Simon had already had some contact with each other because, in Luke 4:38–39, we read that Jesus had been in Simon's house, where he had healed Simon's mother-in-law.

Let's explore further...

Take a moment to imagine the geography. Lake Gennesaret is Luke's name for Lake Galilee. It had good fish stocks, and fishing was a significant industry in the area. Fishermen would have worked in family or small community partnerships, and you can find echoes of this arrangement in the passage. Night time was usually the prime time for catching fish.

A crowd had gathered to 'hear God's message'. Simon was there, along with other fishermen, cleaning their nets. For him, the words of Jesus were about to turn an ordinary day into an extraordinary one. We can imagine Simon being torn when Jesus told him to put the boat out into the deep water. His fisherman's instinct told him that putting the boat out in the daytime after a failed night's fishing was pointless, but Jesus' request clearly carried authority (Simon called Jesus 'Master') and prompted him into obedience. The catch, when it came, was abundant—so much so that the weight of the fish threatened to sink two boats.

The whole experience had a profound effect on Simon. It caused him to recognize something very significant both about Jesus (addressing him now as 'Lord') and about himself (a deep sense of his own unworthiness). Jesus' response, though encouraging, was also hugely demanding. Although he reassured Simon ('Don't be afraid'), it did not allow him to go back to how things were, but instead placed the most challenging call on his life. Simon, along with James and John, 'left everything' to follow Jesus.

So can it be said that this is a passage for young children? Yes, indeed. As with all stories, there are aspects that may not resonate with very young children, but this leaves scope for later fruitful and meaningful encounters with the story.

The story

See notes on storytelling materials on page 20.

> **You will need:**
> * The story basket
> * The sand-coloured story cloth
> * Blue fabric for the lake
> * A boat
> * A net (such as a fruit or vegetable net)
> * Some fish (wood or Fimo) in a basket, one for each person if possible
> * The figures of Jesus, twelve disciples and three or four women, in a basket

Setting up the story

(Bring out the story basket and create an air of mystery as you open it.) I wonder who or what our story is going to be about today? I wonder where our story will be? *(Lay out the sand-coloured story cloth.)*

Maybe it's not all sand. *(Bring out the blue fabric.)* Where could this be in our story?

How could we get from here *(point to the right-hand edge of the water)* to here *(move hand to the other side)*, or from here to here? *(Move hand in opposite direction. Talk about the suggestions the group make, such as paddling, swimming, in a boat and so on.)*

(Place the boat on the water.) We've got a boat in our story basket. *(Move the boat around on the water. Talk about their experiences of being in a boat.)*

(Rest the boat on the right-hand edge of the water.) This boat belonged to a man called Simon. *(Place a figure for Simon in the boat.)*

Simon was a fisherman: his job was to catch fish. He would take his boat out at night time into the middle of the lake *(move Simon's boat into the middle of the water)*, then he would throw over a big net *(take out the net and lay it over the side of the boat)*, hoping that lots of fish would get caught in the net, but sometimes he didn't catch anything. *(Hold up the empty net, and lay it across the boat. Move the boat back to the side and then sit back and view the story cloth.)*

So… some water, a boat and a fishing net. *(Touch or point to the different parts as you remind children of the features.)* I think we've got everything we need to start. Are you ready for our story?

Telling the story

Once there was a man who was just like God. His words were like God's words, his thoughts were like God's thoughts, and everything he did was what God would have done. This man was Jesus. *(Take Jesus from story basket and rest him on the palm of your hand.)*

One day, Jesus was standing by a lake, teaching people about God. But there were so many people that he got into one of the boats on the edge of the water. It was Simon's boat. *(Put Jesus into Simon's boat.)*

When he had finished teaching, Jesus said to Simon, 'Row the boat out into the deep water and let your nets down to catch some fish.'

Simon said, 'Master, we have worked hard all night long and have not caught a thing. But if you tell me to, I will let the nets down.' *(Move the boat into the middle and lay the net over the far side of the boat.)*

When they did this, they caught so many fish… *(bring out the basket of fish and invite everyone to put a fish in the net)* they caught so many fish that their nets were beginning to break!

They called to the men in the other boat to come and help them—and the boats started to sink! *(Shake the boat gently.)*

They were all amazed at what they saw.

(Change the tone of your voice.) Then Simon knelt down in front of Jesus and said, 'Lord, don't come near me, for I am not a good man!'

But Jesus said to Simon, 'Do not be afraid. From now on you will bring in people for me instead of fish.'

When Simon had brought the boat back *(move the boats to the edge)*, he left everything and became one of Jesus' closest friends. *(Take the figures for Jesus and Simon out of the boat and move them to start a line along the top side of the lake.)*

Jesus had twelve men who became his special

friends: there was Simon, James and John, who were also fishermen. *(Place a figure down in the line each time you say a name.)* Then there was Andrew, who was Simon's brother, Philip, Bartholomew, Matthew, Thomas, another James, and another Simon, and Judas, and another man called Judas. And there were some women who were also special friends and who helped to look after them all. *(Bring out the women figures and place them with the disciples.)*

Talking about the story

✪ Talk about which part of the story the children liked best.

✪ Was there anything they did not like?

✪ Where would they like to be in the story? *(If possible, have a basket of spare figures so that they can put themselves in the story.)*

✪ What is it like to be one of Jesus' special friends?

Prayer

Before you pray the prayer, talk about whether people in the group would like to be one of Jesus' special friends.

Dear Jesus, thank you that we can be your special friends here in… Help us to be good friends to you. Amen

Individual craft activity

Paper plate fish mobiles

For each child you will need:
✳ A paper plate with a shape cut away for the mouth (see diagram)
✳ Three pre-cut fin shapes for each fish (see template on page 66)
✳ A length of shirring elastic
✳ A message label saying 'Jesus helped Simon to catch lots of fish'
✳ Crayons and sticky tape (for the group as a whole)

Colour in an eye on the fish body. Stick the fin shapes on the top and bottom of the fish. Use a third shape for the tail. Stick the message label in the middle of the fish

and attach the shirring elastic to the back of the fish with sticky tape. Encourage the group to hang the fish from a ceiling or door frame where it will bounce up and down.

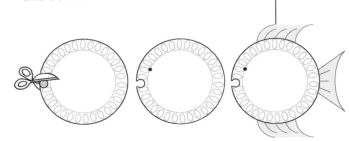

Group craft activity

Friends of Jesus poster

Use a large sheet of paper (the size will depend on the size of your group) and write or print in the middle, 'We can all be friends of Jesus'. Pre-cut simple people figures out of paper, enough for everyone in the group.

Encourage everyone to colour in a picture of themselves, perhaps in their favourite clothes. Stick all the people shapes around the message label.

Snack time

Fish-shaped cakes

Using your own recipe or the one below, make tray bakes of plain sponge cake to cut into fish shapes.

You will need:
225g self-raising flour; 225g butter or margarine; 225g caster sugar; 4 eggs; two tablespoons milk; icing sugar and a selection of cake decorations; mixing spoon or hand-held mixer; mixing bowl; baking parchment or greaseproof paper; Swiss roll tin; wire rack.

Place all the ingredients (except the icing sugar and cake decorations) into the mixing bowl and mix to a smooth batter. Line the Swiss roll tin with baking parchment or greaseproof paper. Spread the mixture evenly in the tin. Bake in a moderate oven at 180°C/350°F/Gas mark 4 for 25–30 minutes. Allow to cool on a wire rack before cutting into fish shapes. Decorate with icing and cake decorations.

The good shepherd

Bible reference: John 10:1–18

Young children may be familiar with the image of Jesus as a shepherd, but they receive this idea usually through hearing the so-called parable of the lost sheep, rather than through Jesus' teaching in John 10:1–18. The concepts expressed in this passage may seem too abstract for young children but it is worth taking a closer look at them.

Let's explore further...

The shepherd as an image for leadership is common in the Bible, and the religious leaders (Pharisees) listening to Jesus would have recognized echoes from Ezekiel's criticism of the 'shepherds' of his day and the prophecy that one day God would come as a very different kind of shepherd (Ezekiel 34). So, just what was Jesus saying here about himself? What was he saying about the religious leaders of his day, and what would his listeners have been thinking? What is a good shepherd like?

Jesus describes the good shepherd as one who calls each of his sheep by name: that is to say, he knows them individually. It is easy to take our names for granted, but they are fundamental in defining who we are: they mark our individuality. To know and use one another's names is not only fundamental in human relationships, but God too, calls us by name. God says, 'I have called you by name; now you belong to me' (Isaiah 43:1), and again, 'I will never forget you… I have written your name on the palms of my hands' (Isaiah 49:15–16, GNB). In baptism, individuals are baptized by name, a sign of God's very personal and particular relationship with them.

The good shepherd goes ahead of his sheep when they are away from the sheepfold. He leads the way and the sheep follow because they know whose voice to trust. The good shepherd goes ahead because he knows where to lead his sheep in order that their needs can be met and to keep them safe. He has their deepest well-being at heart.

The good shepherd 'lays down his life' for the sheep. Such is the love of the good shepherd for his sheep that he will risk his very life for them. Here we have a forward glimpse, knowing that Jesus will indeed lay down his life for all his sheep.

So can it be said that this is a passage for young children? Although some of the ideas are too abstract for young children, when it is narrated alongside the visual 'telling' with the figures, children glean far more than we may anticipate. Sophia Cavalletti[1] believes that this is a key passage for young children: its portrayal of Jesus as the good shepherd meets a critical need for them at this particular period—the need to feel safe, secure and protected. Cavalletti quotes one three-year-old who said, 'The good shepherd is like my mummy; he helps me, takes me across the street; he takes danger away.'

See notes on storytelling materials on page 20.

You will need:

* The story basket
* The sand-coloured story cloth
* Green fabric for grass
* A basket of wooden bricks, including a rectangular brick for the gate
* Figures of Jesus, a shepherd, a hired worker, six sheep and a wolf

---

Setting up the story

(Bring out the story basket and create an air of mystery as you open it.) I wonder who or what our story is going to be about today? I wonder where our story will be? *(Lay out the sand-coloured story cloth.)*

Maybe it's not all sand; maybe there's something else. *(Take out the green fabric and talk about what it might be. Then lay it down at the top end of the story cloth, in the middle.)*

Let's see what else is in the basket. *(Bring out the basket of bricks.)* What might these bricks be? *(Play with some possibilities, then make them into a closed square on the green felt, without using the rectangular brick.)*

What might this be? Does anything or anyone live here? *(Allow time for suggestions.)* Is there anything in the basket that might stay in here? *(Place four sheep in the sheepfold.)* So it's a sheepfold—a place where sheep can be kept safely.

How do they get inside if they are outside, or outside if they are inside? *(Use your fingers to show, for example, climbing over the side, tunnelling underneath and so on.)*

Maybe it needs a doorway or a gateway! *(Replace some bricks with the one rectangular brick.)*

Do the sheep need anyone to look after them? *(Allow time for suggestions.)* There might be a shepherd in the story basket. *(Place the shepherd to the right of the gate of the sheepfold.)*

Is there anything else in here that we need? Perhaps some more sheep. Maybe some sheep don't live in the sheepfold; maybe they live somewhere else. *(Place two sheep at different*

points around the edge of the story cloth and then sit back and view the cloth.)*

So… some grass, a sheepfold, some sheep and a shepherd. *(Touch or point to the different parts as you remind the children of the features.)* I think we've got everything we need to start. Are you ready for our story?

Telling the story

Once there was a man who was just like God. His words were like God's words, his thoughts were like God's thoughts and everything he did was what God would have done. This man was Jesus. *(Take Jesus from the story basket and rest him on the palm of your hand. Then lay Jesus at the edge of the story cloth in front of you.)*

People who came close to Jesus wanted to know who he was. One day, he tried to tell them.

He began by telling them a story about shepherds: 'The shepherd always goes into the sheepfold through the gate. *(Open the 'gate' and move the shepherd to the middle of the entrance.)* Anyone who climbs in another way… *(walk your fingers over the top left corner)* is like a robber.

'The shepherd calls his own sheep by name and they hear his voice. He leads them out. *(Move the shepherd outside the sheepfold. Bring out the sheep one at a time, and close the gate.)*

'When he has brought out all his sheep through the gate, he goes ahead of them, and the sheep follow because they know his voice. The sheep wouldn't follow a stranger because they don't know the stranger's voice.' *(As you are saying this, move the shepherd and sheep in a line, with the shepherd in front; then move them to the middle of the story cloth and round back to the sheepfold. Move the sheep into the sheepfold, leaving the gate open and the shepherd on the outside.)*

But then Jesus said, 'I am the gate for the sheep. *(Say this in a quizzical kind of way. Replace the shepherd figure with the figure for Jesus and lay it across the gate.)* Whoever comes in through me will be safe. *(Walk your fingers over Jesus.)* A robber wants to hurt the sheep, but I have come so that my sheep may have life, and have it fully.' *(Stand Jesus upright by the gateway.)*

Jesus said, 'I am the good shepherd. *(Touch the*

Jesus figure. Then stand Jesus by the 'gate'. Move the Jesus figure and the sheep in a line to the middle of the story cloth, as you did before, but stop in the middle of the story cloth.)

'The good shepherd gives his life for his sheep.

'Someone else might not look after the sheep in the same way (bring out the hired worker and replace Jesus with him; leave Jesus on the edge of the story cloth) because the sheep don't belong to him.

'When he (emphasize 'he') sees the wolf coming (bring out the wolf and place it near the sheep), he runs away (move the hired worker quickly back into the story basket) and the wolf snatches the sheep and the sheep scatter (scatter the sheep). But the good shepherd would give his own life to save the sheep. (Stand the Jesus figure between the wolf and the sheep and move the sheep closer to the good shepherd.)

'I am the good shepherd. (Touch the Jesus figure.) I know my sheep and they know me, just as the Father knows me and I know the Father.' (Move the Jesus figure and the sheep back to the sheepfold. Close the 'gate' with the Jesus figure on the outside.)

'I have other sheep that do not belong to this sheepfold. I must bring them also, and they will listen to my voice. (Move the Jesus figure to the sheep outside on the edge of the story cloth. Bring each sheep to the sheepfold. Close the gate of the sheepfold.)

'So there will be one flock (circle hand over the sheepfold) and one shepherd.' (Touch the Jesus figure.)

Talking about the story

✪ Talk about which part of the story the children liked best.
✪ Was there anything they did not like?
✪ Where would they like to be in the story? (If possible, have a basket of spare figures so that they can put themselves in the story.)
✪ What names might the sheep have?
✪ Who, for the children, are 'good shepherds'?

 Prayer

Before you pray the prayer, ask if there is anyone they know who would like to feel close to the good shepherd.

Dear Jesus, thank you that you are the good shepherd. Thank you that you know each one of us by name and that we can know you. Please be close to... Amen

Individual craft activity

Good shepherd mobiles

For each child you will need:
✱ A round paper plate with three holes punched along the bottom
✱ A picture of a shepherd (see template on page 67)
✱ Three sheep cut from white card (see template on page 67)
✱ Cotton wool
✱ Three lengths of coloured wool with which to hang the sheep from the bottom of the plate, and one length to make a loop at the top for hanging
✱ A message label saying, 'The good shepherd knows his sheep and they know him'
✱ Glue sticks, crayons and sticky tape (for the group as a whole)

Colour in the good shepherd picture if desired. Stick the picture on to the middle of the paper plate. Stick cotton wool on to the sheep. Using sticky tape, fasten a length of wool to the back of each sheep. Thread the other end of each length through the holes at the bottom of the plate and secure with a knot. Make a hanging loop with another piece of wool and fasten it at the top of the plate on the back.

Group craft activity

A footstep banner

Make a banner using part of a roll of lining wallpaper (not ready-pasted). Glue a picture of the good shepherd at one end. Cut out and stick everyone's footprints on to the banner. You could make these by 'foot printing' in paint or, for a less messy option, draw around everyone's feet on sugar paper. Arrange the prints on the banner as if going towards the good shepherd, and write everyone's names on their own footprints. Add the label saying, 'The good shepherd calls each of his sheep by name and leads them out'.

Foot printing in paint may seem daunting but can be done very efficiently with appropriate preparation. Lay down a large plastic sheet (an old shower curtain works well). Prepare a sequence that everyone will follow. Have available various colours of ready-mixed paints and put the paint on to trays or in small bowls. Have pieces of sponge ready. In a line along the plastic sheeting, set out the paint and the sponges, then the paper, then a bowl of water, soap (consider any problems with allergies or infections, such as verrucas) and a towel. Place a chair near the paint and one near the bowl of water. Involve the carers in helping. In turn, each child sits on the chair: use the sponges to dab paint on their feet, then help them stand on the paper to make their footprints, then help them on to the chair to have their feet washed.

Heart shaped cakes

Make up a sponge cake mixture (see page 31) and bake it in a Swiss roll tin. Use a heart-shaped cutter to make the cakes. Children could decorate their cake before they eat it.

Note
1   S. Cavalletti, *The Religious Potential of the Child* (Catechesis of the Good Shepherd, 1992), ch. 3.

Jesus blesses little children

Bible reference: Mark 10:13–16

This incident has long been rendered as a rather cosy story: parents bring their children to Jesus to be blessed, the disciples want to send them away but Jesus insists with the words 'Let the children come to me', and Jesus then takes them in his arms to bless them. Jesus' attitude and actions have been seen as an example of how the church ought to welcome children.

Let's explore further...

Emotions run high in this passage. People were bringing little children to be blessed by Jesus (eagerly and excitedly, or with anxiety and trepidation?) but the disciples, taking the role of modern-day bouncers, spoke sternly to them and tried to stop them. No doubt they had Jesus' best interests at heart, but it was the disciples with whom Jesus was 'indignant' (v. 14, NIV). There is a tendency to imagine Jesus as just being a bit 'miffed' by the situation, but one dictionary definition renders 'indignant' as 'annoyed, infuriated, exasperated'—and these were his closest friends! They were still failing to understand him and the nature of the kingdom that he was proclaiming. Previously, when the disciples had been arguing about which of them was the greatest (Mark 9:33–37), Jesus had set a child among them as a symbol of the 'upside down values' of the kingdom of God. Now they were turning away the very people whom he had shown as an example of greatness. In stark rejection of their attitude, we see that Jesus took the children in his arms and blessed them.

In between the disciples' act of exclusion and his act of inclusion, Jesus makes two statements about children as signs of the kingdom of God. First of all, he said that the kingdom of God belongs to 'such as these' (that is, the children: v. 14, NIV). By this he shows that God's way of doing things belongs to those, like the little children in their midst, who are weak, vulnerable, powerless and marginalized—in direct contrast to the self-important attitude being displayed by the disciples. Secondly, if anyone wants to enter the kingdom of God, they must receive it like a child. Entrance into the kingdom is not through power, status, knowledge or wealth (look ahead to Mark 10:17–31 for more on wealth); indeed, those qualities have no place in it. Adults often have to learn how to live without these things, whereas children don't yet know what it is to have them.

So, can it be said that this is a story about the way Jesus cares for children? Yes, and much more. The story speaks powerfully of children as signs of the kingdom of God and, consequently, of their place in that kingdom.

The story

See notes on storytelling materials on page 20.

> **You will need:**
> ✳ The story basket
> ✳ The sand-coloured story cloth
> ✳ The fabric for the road
> ✳ A basket of bricks, enough to make the base of a house
> ✳ Figures of Jesus, four disciples, five children, and three parents

Setting up the story

(Bring out the story basket and create an air of mystery as you open it.) I wonder who or what our story is going to be about today? I wonder where our story will be? *(Lay out the sand-coloured story cloth.)*

How might you get from there *(point to the right-hand edge of the story cloth)* to there *(move your hand across to the other side of the story cloth)*, or from there to there? *(Reverse movement. Talk about the possibilities.)*

We need a road! *(Bring out the strip of fabric for the road, and lay it across the story cloth.)*

I wonder if anyone is going to travel along this road? *(Walk your fingers up and down the road and give the children time to suggest who might do so.)*

We've got some people in our story basket— some children and some grown-ups. Maybe they are going to travel along this road. *(Take out the children and 'parents' and place them on the road on the right-hand edge of the story cloth. Talk about where they might be going and who they might be going to see.)*

We've got some bricks in the basket. What might these be in the story? *(Talk about possibilities.)* They could be a house. *(Make the base of a house, adjacent to the road, to your left, with a gap for the entrance on one side.)*

I wonder who lives in the house. Let's see… *(Take the disciple figures out and place them in the house.)* Who might these people be? *(Sit back and view the story cloth.)*

So… a road, some children and some grown-ups

about to go somewhere, a house with some more people in it. *(Touch or point to the different parts as you remind children of the features.)* I think we've got everything we need to start. Are you ready for our story?

Telling the story

Once there was a man who was just like God. His words were like God's words, his thoughts were like God's thoughts and everything he did was what God would have done. This man was Jesus. *(Take Jesus from the story basket and rest him on the palm of your hand.)*

One day, Jesus was talking to his disciples, his special friends. *(Put Jesus in the house with the disciples.)*

People were bringing little children to Jesus. *(Move parent figures and the children along the road towards the house. Stop the parents a little away from the house and move only the children nearer the house.)*

They wanted Jesus to bless the children.

When the disciples saw them coming, they told them off *(move two disciples to block the doorway)* and tried to stop them. *(Put your hand in the air with the palm outwards, in a 'stopping' gesture.)*

But when Jesus saw this, he was cross. He said, 'Let the children come to me! Don't try to stop them. People who are like these little children belong to the kingdom of God.' *(Move the disciples to the edges of the house.)*

(Move Jesus to a place on his own in the middle of the house.) 'Listen,' Jesus said. 'This is really important. Whoever does not accept God's way of doing things, in the way that a little child does, will never enter it.'

Then Jesus took the children in his arms, and blessed them by placing his hands on them. *(Move children forward around Jesus, make a blessing gesture on them, and then line the children on either side of Jesus.)*

Talking about the story

✪ Talk about which part of the story the children liked best.

✪ Was there anything they did not like?

✪ Where would they like to be in the story? *(If possible, have a basket of spare figures so that they can put themselves in the story.)*

Prayer

The children came very close to Jesus and he placed his hand on them and blessed them. Do you think they felt special when he did this? *(If it is part of your church's practice, you could talk about the minister blessing children at the Communion rail.)* Ask if they know anyone who might want Jesus to bless them.

Dear Jesus, thank you that we can think of you placing your hand on our heads and blessing us. Please bless… Amen

Individual craft activity

Paper chain of children to dress

For each child you will need:

✳ A paper chain of people, made by folding a piece of A4 paper into four, concertina-style, then drawing a person on the top sheet, making sure that the arms reach to the folds on either side. Cut around the outline, being careful not to split the chain where the people meet at the folds

✳ A strip of A4 card, about 4cm wide, on which is written/printed: 'Let the children come!'

✳ Cut-outs of T-shirts and shorts from self-adhesive felt or vivelle

✳ Glue sticks and crayons (for the group as a whole)

Stick the T-shirts and shorts on the paper chain people. Add features on the face with crayons. Stick the message strip across the bottom of the chain. If you concertina-fold the card slightly, the chain of children will stand on their own.

Group craft activity

Patchwork quilt

You will need:

✳ Paper in different colours

✳ Crayons

Cut out squares of different coloured paper with sides of about 15cm. Ask the children to use plastic or wax crayons to draw a picture of themselves, to fit the piece of paper.

Make up a patchwork quilt by gluing the squares on to a background sheet. Leave some spaces clear for the Bible verse: 'Jesus took the children in his arms and blessed them' (Mark 10:16).

Snack time

Make or buy biscuits in the shape of gingerbread people. Children can decorate them before they eat them.

You will need:

300g plain flour; a pinch of salt; 1 teaspoon baking powder; 1 teaspoon ground ginger; 100g butter or margarine; 100g soft brown sugar; 2 eggs; 60g golden syrup; mixing bowl; mixing spoon or hand-held mixer; small rolling pins; baking parchment or greaseproof paper; flour; mini chocolate or candy sweets, or currants.

Put the flour, salt, baking powder and spice into a bowl. Rub in the butter or margarine, then stir in the sugar. Beat the eggs with the golden syrup and add to the mixture. Mix well either by hand or with a hand-held mixer.

Have a surface ready for rolling with pieces of well-floured baking parchment or greaseproof paper. The dough should be rolled out to about 5mm thickness and then the biscuits can be cut out with people-shaped cutters. Decorate with mini chocolate or candy sweets or currants.

Place each biscuit on a square of baking parchment, marked with the child's name, then put the biscuits on a baking sheet and bake them. If you have no kitchen facilities, the children could take their biscuits home unbaked, with instructions on how to bake them at home. The biscuits will need to be baked in an oven pre-heated to Gas Mark 3/325°F/170°C for about 18 minutes.

NB: Make sure the children wash their hands before the activity. If you have no water connection, have available a plastic washing-up bowl, water warmed in a kettle, some soap and towels. As with any food activity, check whether any child has allergies, and, as the biscuit recipe has egg in it, make sure the children don't eat the raw dough.

Jesus heals an older woman and a young girl

Bible reference: Mark 5:21–43

When we tell children the account of the raising of Jairus' daughter, we often tell it as a self-contained story and omit the healing of the woman with a haemorrhage (vv. 25–34), as if it is superfluous to the 'main' account of Jairus and his daughter (vv. 21–24, 35–43). But the two accounts are inextricably connected and should be regarded as a whole.

Let's explore further...

Far from being incidental, the woman is a key part of the passage because of the way in which she and Jairus stand in marked contrast with each other: Jairus is named; she is anonymous. Jairus has status and power as the head of his house and of the synagogue; the woman's medical condition renders her marginalized (she was regarded as 'unclean') and poor (she has spent all her money on medical bills). For twelve years Jairus has been blessed with the life of his daughter; for twelve years the woman's life has been diminished by her condition. Jairus goes to Jesus openly and speaks to him face to face; the woman comes up behind Jesus and attempts to touch his cloak secretly. Jairus can speak out in the interests of his daughter; the woman has no one to speak for her.

Yet, for all their differences, there is also a sense of solidarity between the two people. Both Jairus and the woman are in desperate need; both fall before Jesus in fear (vv. 22, 33); both come in faith that Jesus can heal and restore. Both will come to know the healing and restoration that they seek, but, in their encounters with

Jesus, both will also be caught up in the unexpected.

For both characters, in Jesus their two worlds collide and all the old values are turned upside down. Jairus, the one accustomed to status and authority, discovers that his needs are no more important than the needs of a poor woman deemed to be 'unclean' and unimportant. The woman discovers that, in the kingdom of God (where life is lived in his way), true healing is found not just in relief from physical symptoms but also in personal acceptance by Jesus, as she stands before him face to face. Jairus, accustomed to prominence and importance, finds himself on the sidelines as the woman, accustomed to being on the margins, becomes the daughter (v. 34, NIV) at the centre of the scene; and both discover that healing and restoration happen at the hands of Jesus but in his time and in his way.

Meanwhile, what of the little girl? Has she become peripheral to the main story? Not at all! The fact that Jesus could raise her to new life from death is a sign of his ultimate God-given authority. The effects of Jesus' intervention were instantaneous: she got up straight away, began to walk about and was ready to eat. There is also something significant about the relationship between Jesus and the girl. Despite the adults who sought to stand between them, Jesus came and spoke to her personally, took her by the hand and called her to new life. She, for her part, responded instantly without hesitation or questioning. Jesus called and the child responded. And, in instructing the parents not to tell anyone, perhaps Jesus was indicating that their proclamation was unnecessary and even misplaced, because the girl's own new life, with all its vitality, was proclamation enough to signify God's glory.

So can it be said that in its entirety this story is suitable for young children? Yes, very much so! Although a story about Jesus ministering to a little girl may seem to be attractive for young children, they have little real appreciation of what Jesus does for the child. Young children have a very limited understanding of death, often confusing it with sleep, and do not yet realize either the permanent state of death or how it affects other people. Therefore, it may not be so appropriate to make this the sole focus of the story. Enabling young children to encounter the passage as Mark constructed it offers other aspects with which they can engage.

NB: Beware of using the word 'sick' with young children when you mean 'poorly' or 'ill'. To a young child, 'sick' means vomit—as I discovered when, in the early stages of working with this story, children were insistent that, in addition to having something to eat, the little girl would need to get washed and have clean pyjamas on.

 The story

See notes on storytelling materials on page 20.

You will need:
* The story basket
* The sand-coloured story cloth
* The fabric for the road
* A basket of bricks, enough to make the base of a house
* A small padded 'mattress' or rug for a bed
* The figures of Jesus, a child figure and two parents (place the family in a small basket), one figure for the older woman (place her in a small basket like the one used for the family), and five or six figures (a mixture of adult and child figures) for the crowd

---

Setting up the story

(Bring out the story basket and create an air of mystery as you open it.) I wonder who or what our story is going to be about today? I wonder where our story will be? *(Lay out the sand-coloured story cloth.)*

How might you get from there *(point to the right-hand edge of the story cloth)* to there *(move your hand across to the other side of the story cloth)*, or from there to there? *(Reverse movement.*

Talk about the possibilities.)

We need a road! *(Bring out the strip of fabric for the road, and lay it across the story cloth.)*

What else is in our story basket? Mmm, some bricks. I wonder what these might make? *(Take out the bricks, talk about possibilities, and then make them into the base of a big house with an opening on one side for the entrance. Build the house to the left of the story cloth, on the side of the road closest to you.)*

It's a big house. Someone important must live here. Let's see who it is.

It's a family—there's a mum, a dad and a girl, their daughter. She's about twelve years old. *(Bring out the basket with the family in it, and place the figures in the house.)*

The dad's name is Jairus, but we don't know the names of the mum and the girl.

Both the dad, Jairus, and the mum are very sad. Their little girl is very ill. *(Place the mattress down in the house and lay the girl on it, with the mum and dad either side of the mattress.)*

I wonder what they can do to help her? *(Children might suggest giving medicine, or going to the doctor. To each suggestion, say that her mum and dad have done that.)* She really is very poorly. She is so poorly that her mum and dad think she might die.

There's someone else who's ill—a woman. We don't know her name either, but she has been ill for a long time, for twelve years. *(Bring out the basket containing the older woman. Place her at the nearside right corner. These two actions help to indicate her 'aloneness' in comparison with the family.)*

I wonder what she can do? *(Let the children suggest possibilities, but draw attention to her limited options. For example, if the children suggest giving her some medicine, explain that she has no money to buy any medicine. When the suggestions are complete, sit back and view the story cloth.)*

So… a road, a large house where Jairus and his family live, a poorly girl and a poorly woman. *(Touch or point to the different parts as you remind children of the features.)* I think we've got everything we need to start. Are you ready for our story?

Reproduced with permission from *Praise and Play!* published by BRF 2009 (978 1 84101 563 7) www.barnabasinchurches.org.uk

Telling the story

Once there was a man who was just like God. His words were like God's words, his thoughts were like God's thoughts and everything he did was what God would have done. This man was Jesus. *(Take Jesus from the story basket and rest him on the palm of your hand.)*

Wherever Jesus went *(place Jesus near the right-hand edge of the story cloth on the far side of the roadway)*, lots of people came to him. *(Place the crowd figures around him.)* They wanted to hear him tell stories, they wanted to hear him teach, and they wanted him to make people who were unwell better.

When Jairus heard that Jesus was nearby *(move Jairus just outside his house)*, he knew what he had to do. *(Move Jairus, as if running, to Jesus.)*

Jairus begged Jesus over and over again, 'My little girl is very ill; she's going to die! Come and place your hands on her so that she will be better and live.'

Jesus set off with Jairus. *(Move Jesus and Jairus partway along the road.)*

As they were going along the road, the woman who had been ill for twelve years crept quietly up to Jesus. She just wanted to touch a bit of Jesus' clothes. That would be enough to make her well again. *(Move a figure up behind Jesus.)* She didn't say anything; she just crept up behind Jesus and touched his coat *(bring the woman right up to Jesus)*, and straight away she knew she was better.

But Jesus knew someone was there, someone who needed him, and he turned *(turn Jesus to the woman)* and saw the woman. She was frightened, but Jesus' face was full of kindness and he said to her, 'You are well. You don't need to worry about this any more.' *(As you say this, lower your hand over the woman as if in a blessing action, then move her to join the crowd.)*

Jesus hadn't forgotten the little girl, but before he could go on to see her some people came and said to Jairus, 'Your daughter has died. Why bother Jesus any more?'

Jesus said to Jairus, 'Don't worry. Just have faith!' And they went on together. *(Move Jesus and Jairus to the entrance to the house.)*

When they got to the house *(place Jesus and Jairus in the house)*, Jesus went to the little girl. *(Move Jesus to the mattress.)* He held her hand and said, 'Little girl, get up!' And straight away the girl got up and began to walk about. *(Stand the girl up and move her around.)*

Her parents were amazed. Jesus ordered them not to tell anyone about what had happened. Then he said, 'Give her something to eat.'

And Jesus left them and went to another place. *(Move Jesus out of the house and along the road, away from the direction in which he had come.)*

Talking about the story

✪ Talk about which part of the story the children liked best.
✪ Was there anything they did not like?
✪ Where would they like to be in the story? *(If possible, have a basket of spare figures so that they can put themselves in the story.)*

 Prayer

Before you pray the prayer, ask the children if they know anyone who is ill at the moment.

Dear Jesus, thank you for the story of how you made the little girl and the older woman well. Please be with all those who are poorly today, especially... Amen

Individual craft activity

A walking puppet

For each child you will need:
* An outline of the puppet figure (see template on page 68) on thin card, with two holes cut at the bottom so that the children can put their fingers through. Using a small circle punch is quickest
* A message label saying, 'Jesus said, "Little girl, get up!" The little girl got straight up and started walking round' (Mark 5:42)
* For the group as a whole: glue sticks, crayons, materials to dress the puppet, such as lengths of wool for hair, vivelle, self-adhesive felt or fabric cut to the shape of the body for clothes

Use crayons to draw features for the face. Add on the 'hair' and the 'clothes'. Stick the message label on the back of the puppet. Show how you can put your fingers through the holes and make the puppet walk.

Group craft activity

Hand-print get well card

Make a hand-print get well card to give to someone who is ill. Fold a large sheet of card in half (the size will depend on the number of children in your group). Write or print the messages. For example, on the front write 'Get Well Soon' and on the inside write 'With love from everyone at Praise and Play'.

Set up hand-printing. Pour ready-mixed paint into dishes or trays and put a piece of household sponge in the middle (this helps to soak up the paint). Work the paint into the sponge. Have a bowl of water, soap (be aware of allergy problems) and towels ready. Each person then presses a hand on to the paint-soaked sponge, then presses on the card, then straight into the bowl of water to have their hands washed. (Alternatively, you can buy sets of hand-painting trays ready prepared from craft shops.)

Let everyone know to whom the card will be sent.

Snack time

A 'get well' plate

Have a selection of food available, such as pieces of apple, orange segments, grapes, carrot sticks, cherry tomatoes, crisps and so on. Explain that Jesus told the girl's parents to give their daughter some food. What would you want to give her from the table? Give each child a small bowl. When they have chosen, they can enjoy their own bowl of food.

The man with a hundred sheep

Bible reference: Luke 15:1–7

Often called the parable of the lost sheep, this passage is frequently presented to children as the story of a sheep who has got lost, and of a shepherd who searches everywhere until he finds it and then brings it safely back home. Children are encouraged to identify God or Jesus with the shepherd and themselves with the lost sheep. But as with so many biblical stories, there is much more to it.

Let's explore further...

The parable of the lost sheep does not stand on its own but within a context (Luke 15:1–2). It was an occasion when Jesus was criticized for eating with tax collectors and sinners. His response was a story, addressed directly to the religious leaders (Pharisees) and the teachers of the Law of Moses (scribes) who were grumbling at him. Jesus told the story in the form of a question: 'If any of you has a hundred sheep, and one of them gets lost, what will you do?'

The last thing a Pharisee or a scribe would want to be was someone who looked after sheep! Shepherds were a much lower class in society and were regarded as unclean because they had to deal with dead sheep on occasions. (As an aside, neither the scribe nor the Pharisee would want to be a woman—the subject of the parable that immediately follows.)

Notice also, contrary to many children's versions of this parable, that the shepherd does not secure his 99 sheep before he sets off to look for the one that is missing; rather, he leaves them in the field (v. 4). This shepherd takes a huge risk for the one sheep that is missing.

The story is often embellished with imaginative details of all the places the shepherd might have searched for the lost sheep. However, the climax of the story then becomes the moment when the shepherd finds the sheep, whereas the concluding verses (vv. 6–7) would suggest that the climax is in the rejoicing and celebration after the sheep has been found. Once, when I told this story, a four- to five-year-old drew a picture of sheep, shepherd's footprints and two circles. He told me that the two circles were trampolines. It must have been some party if there were two trampolines!

So can it be said that this is a reassuring story about a shepherd going to great lengths to find his missing sheep? Yes, but it is also much more. Perhaps this story is as much about how those in leadership exercise their shepherding roles as it is about lost sheep. The shepherd in the parable is one who actively searches out the sheep that is lost until he finds it (v. 4), and then rejoices in its restoration. The story opens another window into the kingdom of God: the way God does things, there is more joy over one person who repents of turning away from God than over 99 people who need no repentance. Which one of you—Pharisees and scribes—is like this kind of shepherd?

The story

See notes on storytelling materials on page 20.

Setting up the story

(Bring out the story basket and create an air of mystery as you open it.) I wonder who or what our story is going to be about today? I wonder where our story will be? *(Lay out the sand-coloured story cloth.)*

And what could this be? I wonder what could be green like this? *(Lay the grass down in the near right-hand corner.)*

Mmm, is there something missing? We've no people or animals. I wonder whether anything or anyone lives here? *(Allow time for the children to give some suggestions.)* Let's see what's in the story basket. *(Bring out the sheep and place them on the grass.)* Some sheep! Sheep live here.

I wonder if the sheep live here by themselves, or if anyone looks after them? *(Place the shepherd figure near the sheep.)*

There are some other things in the basket. What could these be? *(Show the coloured shapes. As you lay them down on the sand-coloured story cloth, make a comment about each one, and talk about what it might be. For example, 'This one has sharp edges…' When all the shapes have been laid down, sit back and view the story cloth.)*

So… some sheep, a shepherd, some grass, and a large area with not much in it but… well, we're not quite sure. *(Touch or point to the different fabric shapes to remind the children of the 'places' in the desert.)* I think we've got everything we need to start. Are you ready for our story?

Telling the story

Once there was a man who was just like God. His words were like God's words, his thoughts were like God's thoughts and everything he did was what God would have done. This man was Jesus. *(Take Jesus from the story basket and lay him in the palm of your hand.)*

Jesus made friends with all kinds of people, but especially he made friends with people who were ill, people who had no money, people who knew that they weren't very good people. But some other people got very cross with him for making friends with the ones who weren't very good, so one day Jesus told them a story. *(Place Jesus in front of you at the edge of the story cloth.)*

'Which one of you, having a hundred sheep… *(sweep hand across the sheep)* and losing one of them… *(place one sheep away from the flock towards the edge of the cloth)* does not leave the rest… *(move the shepherd away from the other sheep)* … and go to look for the lost sheep?'

Is it here? *(Move the shepherd around the cloth, stopping at various 'places' as if looking for the sheep.)* Is it here?

'You look and look, until you find it. *(Place the shepherd next to the sheep.)* When you have found it, you put the sheep on your shoulders and give a great big cheer. *(Bring the shepherd and the sheep towards the flock, but place them a little way from the flock, with the sheep by the shepherd.)*

'When you come home, you call together all your friends and neighbours, saying, "Celebrate with me… *(take out the table from the story basket and place it on the cloth so that the shepherd is standing at the table with the sheep next to him)*, for I have found my sheep that was lost."' *(Raise the sheep slightly. Take out the people and place some around the table and others as if going to the table.)*

Then Jesus said something else. *(Use a curious tone of voice.)* He said, 'I tell you, there will be more joy in heaven over one person who says sorry for turning away from God than over 99 people who do not need to say sorry.'

Talking about the story

❂ Talk about which part of the story the children liked best.

❂ Was there anything they did not like?

❂ Where would they like to be in the story? *(If possible, have a basket of spare figures so that they can put themselves in the story.)*

❂ Talk about times when they have felt lost.

 ### Prayer

Before you pray the prayer, ask if there is anyone the children know who would like to be close to Jesus.

Dear Jesus, thank you that you always want to be close to us. Help us to stay close to you. Today, please come close to... Amen

Individual craft activity

Party hats

> **For each child you will need:**
> * A semicircle cut from an A2 sheet of sugar paper (see instructions below)
> * Sheep-shaped cut-outs (see template on page 67). You could use vivelle or self-adhesive felt to give variety in texture
> * Streamers made from strips of different coloured crêpe paper
> * A message label saying, 'Let's celebrate! I've found my lost sheep'
> * Glue sticks, crayons, a stapler and sticky tape (for the group as a whole)

Each A2 sheet of sugar paper will make two hats. Cut the largest circle possible from each sheet. An easy way to do this is to fold a sheet of paper in half, then in half

again, so that it is one quarter the original size (it is now A4 size). Using a ruler, make marks in an arc 21cm from the corner fold. Cut along the arc through all four layers. Then fold the circle in half and cut along the fold line.

The semicircle of paper will bend around to form a cone: the curved edge will become the base of the hat and the straight edge will be fastened at the back.

Decorate one side of the semicircle by sticking on the sheep-shaped cut-outs. Glue the message label at the base of the hat in the middle. Glue the ends of the streamers along the straight edge. Form a cone-shaped hat by bending the paper round and fastening the outer points of the straight edge together with a staple. Overlap as much as is needed to fit the particular child's head. Attach a piece of sticky tape over the points of the staple inside the hat for safety.

Group craft activity

Good shepherd poster

In the middle of a large sheet of paper, glue a picture of the good shepherd and a sheep (see templates on page 67). Give everyone a paper circle and ask them to draw a happy face. Stick the faces around the shepherd and the sheep. Make a label saying, 'The shepherd said, "Let's celebrate! I've found my lost sheep"' (Luke 15:6).

Snack time

Shepherd's smiley face crackers

Spread large round crackers or round toast biscuits with cream cheese. Cut grapes in half for eyes, cut cherry tomatoes in half for noses (place flat side down), and use apple slices for mouths.

NB: Beware of food allergies concerning wheat or milk.

Jesus calms a storm

Bible reference: Mark 4:35–41

Sudden squalls of the kind described in this story are a feature of the Sea of Galilee: a strong wind whips up and the sea quickly becomes very rough with big waves tossing any boats that are caught in it. This particular squall must have been especially rough because it challenged the skills of those disciples who were experienced fishermen.

Let's explore further...

Faith and trust are key features of this story. Psalm 4:8 says, 'I can lie down and sleep soundly because you, Lord, will keep me safe.' The capacity to sleep peacefully and untroubled was a sign of complete trust in the protective presence of God, and Jesus could do this in a boat that was being tossed around in a great storm. Contrast him with the disciples, who wake Jesus in panic. The disciples ask, 'Don't you care?' Jesus responds, 'Don't you have any faith?'

To the Jewish people, the sea was a symbol of chaos, of evil powers threatening destruction. In the Old Testament, we read of occasions when God's ultimate authority was displayed by the power he exercised over water: in the story of creation, God worked to bring order from the swirling mass of water; he parted the waters of the Reed Sea to form a dry path for Moses and the Israelites to walk through; in Psalm 89:9 the writer praises God with the words, 'You rule the roaring sea and calm its waves.' Against the background of these kinds of pictures, the story in Mark's Gospel tells of a fishing boat (probably rather insubstantial) carrying Jesus and his terrified disciples as they were tossed and buffeted around on a squally sea. At Jesus' command, the wind ceases, the waves calm down and the disciples

ask one another, 'Who is this? Even the wind and the waves obey him!' Who indeed! Jesus will ask this question of them in Mark 8:29, by which time Peter will have the answer: 'You are the Messiah!'

There are a number of Bible stories that speak of God providing a place of safety in the face of dangerous waters: the ark that carried Noah, his family and the animals; the cradle that floated on the River Nile carrying the infant Moses; even the great fish that kept Jonah safe. This fishing boat, tossed around by the wind and waves, also becomes an 'ark' because of the presence of Jesus.

So is this a story about Jesus' amazing power? Yes, and so much more. But for young children it is a story that speaks of safety, security and reassurance in the presence of Jesus, and it offers another window into the kingdom of God. In the way that God does things, all are ultimately safe.

The story

See notes on storytelling materials on page 20.

You will need:
* The story basket
* The sand-coloured story cloth
* Blue fabric for the lake
* A boat
* Figures of Jesus, and as many disciple figures as will fit in the boat

Setting up the story

(Bring out the story basket and create an air of mystery as you open it.) I wonder who or what our story is going to be about today? I wonder where our story will be? *(Lay out the sand-coloured story cloth.)*

Maybe it's not all sand; there's something else. *(Take out the piece of blue fabric.)* What could this be in our story? *(Lay down the blue fabric in the middle of the story cloth. Talk about possibilities.)*

I wonder how you might get from this side to that side, or from that side to this side? *(Move hand from one side of lake to the other. Talk about the possibilities: you might paddle—use your fingers to demonstrate—or swim or get in a boat.)*

There's a boat in our story basket. *(Place boat on water.)* I wonder if you have ever been in a boat? *(Talk about experiences.)*

Was it calm like this…? *(Move the boat gently on the water.)*

Or was it like this…? *(Move the boat as if being tossed about.)*

Sometimes, on the water, it can get very stormy. The wind blows and the waves get really big. I wonder how it feels to be in a boat when the wind blows and the waves get really big? *(Leave the boat at the right-hand edge of the lake, then sit back and view the story cloth.)*

So… a lake and a boat. *(Touch or point to the different parts as you remind children of the features.)* I think we've got everything we need to start. Are you ready for our story?

Telling the story

Once there was a man who was just like God. His words were like God's words, his thoughts were like God's thoughts and everything he did was what God would have done. This man was Jesus. *(Take Jesus from the story basket and rest him on the palm of your hand.)*

Once, when it was nearly night time, Jesus *(place Jesus by the boat)* and his special friends, his disciples, were by the lake. *(Place the disciples by Jesus.)*

Jesus said, 'Let us go across to the other side of the lake'. They got into the boat *(place Jesus and disciples in the boat)* and set out across the lake. *(Move the boat into the middle of the lake.)*

Jesus went to sleep on a cushion at one end of the boat. *(If practical, lie Jesus down at one end of the boat.)*

But a great wind started to blow, and the waves were so big that water came into the boat. *(Lift the boat and rock it as if being tossed around on the waves.)*

Jesus' friends, his disciples, were frightened. They woke Jesus and said to him, 'Teacher, don't you care that we are about to drown?'

Jesus woke up *(stand Jesus up in the boat with one hand, while keeping the boat rocking with the other)* and spoke firmly. He told the wind to stop blowing and said to the waves, 'Be quiet!'

Straight away, the wind stopped blowing and the water was very calm. *(Bring the boat to a gentle movement.)*

Then Jesus said to his friends *(turn Jesus around)*, 'Why were you afraid? Don't you have any faith?'

The disciples were amazed. They said to each other, 'Who is this?' *(Touch Jesus.)* 'Even the wind and the waves obey him!'

Talking about the story

☺ Talk about which part of the story the children liked best.
☺ Was there anything they did not like?
☺ Where would they like to be in the story? *(If possible, have a basket of spare figures so that they can put themselves in the story.)*

Prayer

Talk together about the kind of things that frighten you.

Dear Jesus, thank you that you are with us when we are frightened. And thank you that you can calm things down when they get too much for us. Amen

Individual craft activity

Moving sail boat pictures

For each child you will need:

* An A4 sheet of light blue card for the background
* A strip of dark blue paper (about 30cm x 9cm) for the sea. Cut a wavy edge along one long side
* Pre-cut shapes for the sailboat: the boat, mast and sail. Cut the boat and mast from card and the sail from paper (see templates on page 69)
* A message label saying, 'Jesus got up and ordered the wind and waves to be quiet. The wind stopped and everything was calm'
* A handle made from a strip of card, about 17cm x 2cm (see template on page 69)
* Split pins. (It helps if, before the children start, you make a hole in both the boat and the background card with a tapestry or darning needle at the point where the split pin will be placed)
* Glue sticks and sticky tape (for the group as a whole)

Glue the dark blue paper along the bottom of the background card to form the sea. Make the sailboat by gluing the sail to the mast and gluing the mast in position on the boat. Stick the handle to the back of the boat so that it sticks out to the right. When positioned on the background card, it should overhang the right-hand edge.

Adult task: push the split pin through the hole in the boat and then through the background card. Open out the pins at the back and cover with sticky tape.

You will now be able to move the handle up and down so that the boat appears to be bobbing on the waves. Glue the message label in the top left-hand corner of the background card.

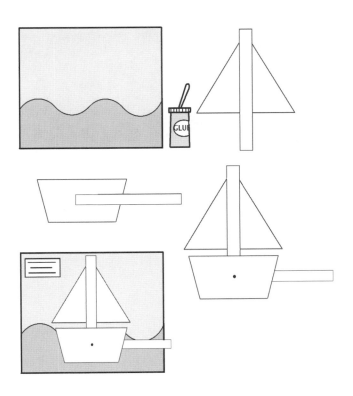

Group craft activity

A collage picture

Make the picture on a large sheet of dark coloured card or stiff paper. Use torn-up strips of light blue, dark blue and green tissue paper for the sea. Use white finger paint for the tops of the waves. Make the base of the boat from a material such as brown corrugated card and the sail from white paper. Make grey paper clouds to stick in the sky.

Add a message label saying, 'Jesus got up and ordered the wind and waves to be quiet. The wind stopped and everything was calm' (Mark 4:39).

Snack time

Sail boat cheese rolls

Cut finger rolls in half lengthways and spread with butter or margarine. To make the sails, cut cheese squares in half to make two triangles. Cut up plastic straws to a suitable length, thread them through the cheese triangle and stick them, upright, into the bread roll.

NB: Be aware especially of wheat or milk allergies.

Jesus feeds a great crowd

Bible reference: John 6:1–15

Miracles are an important feature of the Gospels, yet some adults are cautious about introducing 'miracle' stories to young children in case they confuse miracles with magic. But magic does not mean quite the same thing to young children as it does to adults. For adults, magic is something that involves trickery or sleight of hand, whereas, for young children, magic means something that they cannot explain. Indeed, much of life is a miracle for young children as they encounter the ever-widening world around them. When this story is told to young children, it is often presented as a 'morality tale' highlighting the sacrificial generosity of the boy, which means that the sense of the miraculous gets pushed to the margins.

Let's explore further...

In John's Gospel, miraculous deeds are called 'signs' because, like signposts, they point the way to who Jesus really is. Later in chapter 6, Jesus will develop in words what he first 'signposts' in action in the feeding of the great crowd, when he says, 'I am the bread that gives life. No one who comes to me will ever be hungry. No one who has faith in me will ever be thirsty' (v. 35). Seen in one way, the account tells of Jesus satisfying the physical hunger of the crowd, but his action also points to himself as the one who satisfies a much deeper kind of hunger in people's spirits.

This account is set at the time of the Jewish festival of Passover (v. 4), during which people of Jewish faith remembered the turning point of their history when God rescued them from slavery in Egypt and brought them through the Reed Sea to the promised land. While they were travelling through the wilderness,

Moses had asked God to help because they had no food, and God had provided manna. Here the people are miraculously fed again, but the food that Jesus offered was a different kind of food, one that would give 'life to the world' (v. 33).

Although the account of Jesus feeding a great crowd appears in all four Gospels, it is only in John's Gospel that the donor of the five loaves and two fish is identified as a boy. There is something of a contrast drawn between the highly sceptical disciple Andrew ('But what good is that with all these people?') and the boy who handed over what he had, in faith that Jesus could do something with it. (If he was old enough to have his own packed lunch, he was no doubt also old enough to realize that five loaves and two fish would not ordinarily feed so many people.)

What Jesus actually did must have been far more than anyone could ever have dreamt of. Have you ever paused to reflect on the amazing abundance in this sign? Not only were all those people fed to 'satisfaction' with five loaves and two fish, but there were twelve baskets of bread left over. This was no modest gesture to 'keep them going' until they got home; this was the sign of a God who gives us abundantly more than we shall ever need. Nor would the generosity have been lost on the people present. Living under Roman occupation, many were short of food; no wonder they looked at Jesus through fresh eyes, saying, 'This must be the Prophet who is to come into the world!' (v. 14). Is this another one of those occasions when we have a window into what the kingdom of God—the way that God does things—is like?

This account ends with the people wanting to make Jesus their king. But what kind of king had they in mind? And what kind of king was Jesus to be?

So can it be said that this is a story about a boy's

sacrificial generosity? Yes, but so much more, even for young children. Here, Jesus turned something ordinary, offered in faith, into something extraordinary. Moreover, although John does not include an account of Jesus sharing the bread and wine in his narrative of the last supper, which covers four whole chapters (John 13—17), here on the mountainside Jesus took the loaves and, when he had given thanks, he distributed them (v. 11)—actions that are still part of Communion worship today.

 ## The story

See notes on storytelling materials on page 20.

> **You will need:**
> * The story basket
> * The sand-coloured story cloth
> * The green fabric for grass
> * Two small plates, five loaves of bread (made of Fimo) and two fish (wood or Fimo)
> * Twelve small baskets
> * Figures of Jesus, a child, four or five figures for the disciples (two of which will stand for Philip and Andrew) and more for the crowd (include adult and child figures: you need enough figures to make it look like a crowd)

Setting up the story

(Bring out the story basket and create an air of mystery as you open it.) I wonder who or what our story is going to be about today? I wonder where our story will be? *(Lay out the sand-coloured story cloth.)*

But is it all sand? Is there something else? *(Take out the green fabric pieces.)* I wonder what could be green like this? *(Lay the green fabric on the story cloth to simulate grass, then sit back and view the story cloth.)*

So… some sand and a lot of grass. *(Touch or point to the different parts as you remind children of the features.)* I think we've got everything we need to start. Are you ready for our story?

Telling the story

Once there was a man who was just like God. His words were like God's words, his thoughts were like God's thoughts and everything he did was what God would have done. This man was Jesus. *(Take Jesus from the story basket and rest him on the palm of your hand.)*

Wherever Jesus went, a large crowd of people followed him, because they had seen how he made people well.

Jesus went up the mountain and sat down *(place Jesus on the sand-coloured story cloth)* with his disciples, his special friends. *(Place the figures for the disciples around Jesus.)*

It was nearly time for the special celebration of the Passover.

When Jesus looked up, he saw a large crowd of people coming to him. *(Place all the other people on the story cloth, mostly on the green fabric but leaving some on the sand. As you place the figures for the crowd, make sure that you place a child figure near one of the disciple figures.)*

Jesus said to Philip *(touch one of the disciple figures to indicate to whom Jesus is talking)*, 'Where will we get enough food to feed all these people?' *(Sweep hand over the crowd.)* Jesus said this to tease Philip. Jesus knew what he was going to do. Philip *(touch the figure for Philip)* said, 'It would take almost a year's wages just to buy only a little bread for each of these people.'

Andrew, another of the disciples, said, 'There is a boy here… *(move forward another disciple figure with the child figure)* who has five small loaves of barley bread *(lay down one plate with five loaves in front of Jesus)* and two fish. *(Lay down the other plate with two fish in front of Jesus.)* But what good is that with all these people?' *(Sweep hand over the crowd.)*

Jesus said, 'Make everyone sit down.' *(Move the figures from the sand to the grass.)* There were so many people—about five thousand altogether.

Then Jesus took the loaves. *(Pick up the plate of loaves with both hands in front of Jesus.)* He gave thanks to God… *(lift up the plate of loaves with both hands)* and shared them with everyone sitting down. *(Move hand around the crowd, stopping momentarily at each group as if giving out bread.)*

Then Jesus did the same with the fish. *(Lift up the plate of fish, then move hand around the crowd, in a similar way.)*

When everyone had eaten as much as they wanted, Jesus said to his disciples, 'Gather up all the leftover bits, so that nothing is lost.' So they gathered up all the bits left over from the bread, and they filled 1, 2, 3, 4, 5, 6, 7, 8, 9, 10, 11, 12 baskets. *(Count out baskets and place them in a line by Jesus.)*

When the people saw what he had done, they said, 'This must be the Prophet who is to come into the world!' *(Raise Jesus slightly from story cloth.)*

Then they tried to make Jesus their king, but he went away to be by himself. *(Take Jesus away.)*

Talking about the story

☻ Talk about which part of the story the children liked best .

☻ Was there anything they did not like?

☻ Where would they like to be in the story? *(If possible, have a basket of spare figures so that they can put themselves in the story.)*

☻ What was it like to receive food from Jesus?

Prayer

Talk about food that the children like.

Dear Jesus, you gave the people all the food they needed. Thank you for all the food we have to eat, especially... Amen

Individual craft activity

Paper lunch baskets

For each child you will need:

✳ A basket shape (see template on page 70) cut from plain coloured basket-weave wallpaper. (If this is not available, use card or stiff paper)

✳ Sugar-paper cut-outs of five loaves and two fish (see template on page 70)

✳ A message label saying, 'Jesus fed everyone'

✳ Glue sticks, wax or plastic crayons (for the group as a whole)

Rub a crayon over one side of the basket. Fold the basket in half and then, on the inside, glue in the five loaves and two fish. Stick the message label on the front of the paper basket.

Group craft activity

A picture display

In preparation, cut pictures of faces from magazines and colour supplements, including men, women and children of a span of ages and from different ethnic origins. Ask everyone to bring a photograph of themselves that they don't mind being used in the picture.

To make the background for the display, cover a large piece of stiff card or mounting board (A3 or A2, depending on number of people working on it and the time available) by gluing on the pictures of faces to make it look like a large crowd. Use the pictures from the magazines and colour supplements first, and, when the board is fairly well covered, cut around the photographs of people from the group. Add these on to the picture display so that they can be easily identified.

When complete, prop the card on a table. In front of the picture, place a basket containing five rolls and two card fish. (Handy hint: if you coat the bread rolls with PVA glue, it will preserve them for a while and stop them going mouldy.) Make a free-standing label saying, 'Jesus took the bread in his hands and gave thanks to God. Then he passed the bread to the people, and he did the same with the fish, until everyone had plenty to eat (John 6:11).'

Snack time

Mini tuna sandwich

Spread slices of bread with butter or margarine and add a filling of mashed tinned tuna. Make into sandwiches. Cut off the crusts and cut the sandwiches into triangles.

NB: Be aware of food allergies.

Jesus and Zacchaeus

Bible reference: Luke 19:1–10

The story of Zacchaeus is another of those stories that we might feel we know well, and it has been familiarized in the much-sung words of the children's chorus 'Zacchaeus was a very little man'. But, because we feel we know the story so well, it is all too easy to rely on our own memory when we come to retell it to children, without going back to the biblical text and first letting the story continue to grow in us.

Let's explore further...

Often, well-known Bible stories are regarded as self-contained units. For this reason, it can be easy to miss their connections with the bigger tapestry that each Gospel writer is weaving. For example, if you read back into Luke 18, you will see that one connecting theme is the difficulty of holding humility and wealth hand in hand ('It's easier for a camel to go through the eye of a needle than for a rich person to get into God's kingdom': v. 25).

In Luke 18:15–17 we are told of children who are signs of God's kingdom, perhaps because they are unencumbered by wealth and possessions. Then, in verses 18–24, Luke tells us about the rich and important man who, though upright in other respects, became very sad when challenged to sell all that he had and to share it out among those who lived in poverty.

Luke also tells of two further and contrasting encounters with Jesus, one by an anonymous poverty-stricken blind man (18:35–43) and the other a rich tax collector named Zacchaeus, both of whom find salvation through Jesus. Looking at the picture as a whole, Zacchaeus shows that it is possible for a wealthy man to get 'through the eye of the needle'—but only after a resolve to change.

Tax collectors were very unpopular. They collected taxes on behalf of the Romans, so they were seen as collaborators. Zacchaeus was a chief tax collector in Jericho, so he would have had a number of tax collectors working for him, who would each pass on what they had collected to him. The system allowed for extra money to be collected at each stage of the process, on top of what the government required, and the potential for corruption was great. Many people were poor and resented the money they had to pay to the Romans, and so also resented the people who collected it. Moreover, the nature of the tax collectors' work meant that they came into contact with Gentiles (people who were not of the Jewish faith), so they were regarded as spiritually unclean.

Despite all this, Jesus picked Zacchaeus out from among the crowd. He spoke to him by name and went to be a guest in his house. Here we have, enacted in the flesh, what Jesus was talking about in his parables about lost things: 'The Son of Man came to look for and to save people who are lost' (Luke 19:10; see ch. 15).

On the surface, this story has a kind of 'happy ever after' feel about it: Zacchaeus has found something of the 'new life' that Jesus came to bring. But is it as comfortable an ending as it might seem? We are not told what happened to Zacchaeus afterwards, but pause with your imagination for a moment. How would he relate now to his local community? Would the people from whom he had previously gathered taxes trust him? Would his tax collector colleagues accept what he had done? Would he still have a job? The 'new life' that Jesus brought may have been very costly for him in more ways than one.

So can it be said that this is a story for young children? Yes, indeed. Children know what it is to be small and have to climb on or up things to see. Many children also know what it feels like to want to be involved but to be pushed back to the margins. The challenge, as always, is to tell the story in such a way that there is scope for it to grow with the children.

 ## The story

See notes on storytelling materials on page 20.

You will need:
* The story basket
* The sand-coloured story cloth
* The fabric for the road
* The basket of bricks
* A tree, made from wood or stout card
* The figure of Jesus, a smaller figure for Zacchaeus, and six to eight people figures for the crowd, placed in a basket

Setting up the story

(Bring out the story basket and create an air of mystery as you open it.) I wonder who or what our story is going to be about today? I wonder where our story will be? *(Lay out the sand-coloured story cloth.)*

How might you get from there *(point to the right-hand edge of the story cloth)* to there *(move your hand across to the other side of the story cloth)*, or from there to there? *(Reverse movement. Talk about the possibilities.)*

We need a road! *(Bring out the strip of fabric for the road, and lay it across the story cloth.)*

Let's see what else we have in the storybasket… some bricks. *(Bring out the basket of bricks.)* What could these be for? *(Talk about possibilities. Form the bricks into the base of a house.)* It could be a house. I wonder who lives in this house?

Maybe this man lives here. *(Bring out the Zacchaeus figure and hold him on the palm of your hand.)* This man's name is Zacchaeus. *(Place Zacchaeus in the doorway of his house.)* His job is to collect money from people—he is a tax collector. Sometimes he takes more money than he should, so now he is rich—he has lots of money.

Is there anything else in our story basket? Yes, a

tree. *(Place the tree to your left, on your side of the road, then sit back and view the story cloth.)*

So… a road, a house where Zacchaeus lives, and a tree. *(Touch or point to the different parts as you remind children of the features.)* I think we've got everything we need to start. Are you ready for our story?

Telling the story

Once there was a man who was just like God. His words were like God's words, his thoughts were like God's thoughts and everything he did was what God would have done. This man was Jesus. *(Take Jesus from the story basket and rest him on the palm of your hand.)*

One day, Jesus was going through the town of Jericho. *(Place Jesus on the road, between the house and the tree.)* Wherever Jesus went, crowds of people came out to see him. *(Bring out the basket of people and arrange the people around Jesus. Leave a gap so that, later, you can move Jesus through the crowd, and Zacchaeus and Jesus from the tree to Zacchaeus' house between the crowd.)*

Zacchaeus was trying to see who Jesus was *(move Zacchaeus so that he is behind the crowd)*, but he was a small man. *(Lift him up and down as if trying to see over the heads of the other people.)*

So he ran ahead and climbed a sycamore tree so that he would see Jesus as he passed by. *(Move Zacchaeus into the tree.)*

When Jesus came to the place *(move Jesus nearer the tree)*, he looked up and said, 'Zacchaeus, hurry and come down, for I must stay at your house today.'

So Zacchaeus hurried down *(move Zacchaeus down the tree and place him by Jesus)* and was happy to welcome him to his house. *(Move both figures through the crowd to Zacchaeus' house.)*

All the people began to grumble: they said, 'Jesus has gone to stay in the house of a man who is not a good man.' *(Circle your hand over the crowd.)*

Zacchaeus stood by Jesus and said *(touch Zacchaeus' head)*, 'I will give half of my property to the poor. And I will now pay back four times as much to everyone I have ever cheated.'

Then Jesus *(touch Jesus' head)* told Zacchaeus that everything would be very different for him and his family from that day onwards.

And Jesus said, 'I came to seek out and save people who are lost.'

Talking about the story

✪ Talk about which part of the story the children liked best.

✪ Was there anything they did not like?

✪ Where would they like to be in the story? *(If possible, have a basket of spare figures so that they can put themselves in the story.)*

✪ Who calls their names, and how it would feel to hear Jesus calling their name?

Prayer

Jesus came close to Zacchaeus. Talk together about anyone they know who might like to have Jesus come close to them.

Dear Jesus, please come close to people who are sad or ill, especially... Show them that you love them, as you love each one of us. Amen

Individual craft activity

A stand-up tree card

For each child you will need:

✻ A piece of A4 card (brown or fawn if possible), folded in half. Cut out a tree shape (see template on page 71) through both thicknesses, making sure you keep the fold joined in both places shown on the template

✻ A piece of brown corrugated paper, cut to the shape of the tree trunk (see template on page 71)

✻ Leaf shapes cut from green paper (see template on page 71)

✻ A circle of skin-coloured paper, about 3cm in diameter

✻ A message label saying, 'Zacchaeus wanted to see Jesus'

✻ Glue sticks and crayons (for the group as a whole)

Stick the brown corrugated paper on to the trunk of the tree on the front of the card. Draw a face and hair on the circle of paper and stick it in the middle of the tree. Stick leaves on the tree, taking care not to cover Zacchaeus' face completely. Stick the message label along the base of the tree.

Group craft activity

Group banner

Use lining wallpaper (not ready-pasted) to make a long rectangular banner shape. Its size will depend on the number in your group. In the middle, write or print, 'Jesus called Zacchaeus by name. How would he call you?'

Cut different-coloured pieces of paper into irregular shapes, large enough to take people's names (you will need one for each person). Write a name on each. Have available a variety of collage materials, such as shapes cut from textured paper, shiny paper, tissue paper, sequin mesh, lengths of wool and so on. Ask everyone to decorate his or her own named paper. Stick the decorated names on to the banner. Help the children to recognize their own.

Snack time

Mini tea party

Have a mini tea party with mini sandwiches, mini fairy cakes and so on.

NB: Be aware of food allergies, especially wheat, milk and nuts.

Jesus appears to Mary Magdalene

Bible reference: John 20:1 and 11–18

Each of the Gospel writers tells the story of the first Easter Day. There are some differences between the accounts, but all confirm that the great stone, which had been placed to seal the tomb, had been rolled away and Jesus' earthly body was no longer present. In John's account, Mary Magdalene was the first to go to the tomb and find that the stone had been moved. Later, she was the first to encounter the risen Jesus close by the empty tomb, and it was she who was charged with telling the disciples all that Jesus had told her.

Let's explore further...

It may be helpful to picture what Jesus' tomb might have been like. Archaeologists have found the remains of many tombs around Jerusalem, consisting of a main chamber, into which the bodies of the deceased would be placed, and a small, low entrance hall, through which anyone would have to stoop to enter (see John 20:5, 11). The tombs were sealed in various ways, including placing large stones against the entrances.

Mary Magdalene must have been on something of an emotional rollercoaster in this story. We can only imagine how she must have felt when she went out to the tomb, early on Sunday morning (v. 1), only to discover that the great stone had been moved. Later, after Simon Peter and John had seen the tomb and gone back to the other disciples, she stood outside weeping—less, perhaps, because of Jesus' death than because the body had disappeared. Abuse of the dead was considered a terrible offence.

Then she discovered two angels sitting inside the tomb where the body of Jesus had been (hardly an everyday event, even in Jesus' time). Her response to

them, and later when she met the figure she supposed to be the gardener, indicates that she thought someone had moved the body to another place. In her distress, she even offered to the 'gardener' to go and get the body back herself, if he could tell her where it was. But then she recognized the voice of the figure who called her by name (here we see echoes of Jesus' words in the passage about the good shepherd, John 10:3–4), and realization dawned instantly.

Mary addressed him as 'Rabboni', not as a question, but as a statement of fact. Rabboni is similar to the word 'rabbi' used elsewhere in the Gospels and, although usually translated as 'teacher', it means literally 'my great one'. Not only was Mary—a woman—the first person to see Jesus alive, but she was then charged with the task of passing on a message from him to the disciples, which is highly significant given that a woman's witness was not given any credence in first-century Judaism. Things had changed! Jesus was raised to new life—not to life as it was before.

We can imagine Mary reaching out when she realizes that Jesus is alive, wanting to hold him in some way. But Jesus resisted, saying, 'Don't hold on to me!' (v. 17). This was because the new relationship was not going to be like the old one. The relationship between Mary and Jesus, as with all the disciples (whom Jesus refers to as 'my brothers' for the first time), had changed. Jesus had not been restored to his old life (in the way that he had brought Lazarus, Jairus' daughter and the widow of Nain's son back to life) but to new life as the forerunner of our new life with God. The disciples would see him now and again, but then he would soon go to his Father, as he had told them he would. For all her previous distress, and her joy and amazement on recognizing the risen Jesus, Mary accepted what Jesus said without any sense of rejection, and went to tell the disciples as she had been instructed.

So can it be said that this is a story for young children? Yes, indeed, but we do have to think seriously about how we convey it. Many people feel uncomfortable about telling the Easter story to young children and, in particular, about telling them of the crucifixion. But the story of Jesus' death and resurrection is at the heart of all that we, as Christians, believe, and we serve our younger children badly if we do not begin to tell them what Easter is about. We cannot tell the story of Jesus appearing to Mary Magdalene without including something of the events that have gone before. The resurrection and the crucifixion are inextricably linked: we cannot tell of one without telling of the other—at least, not without markedly diminishing their significance. Of course, we can tell of the crucifixion without going into the kind of graphic detail that would frighten a young child.

We have to be careful not to reduce the account simply to a sad face/happy face story. At one level, Mary's sadness at the beginning of the story did change to joy when she met the risen Jesus, but we can leave children with an impression that the resurrection in some way 'undoes' the crucifixion: Mary has Jesus back, so everything is all right and they can be happy again, just as they were before Jesus died. It is important to convey that Jesus was raised to *new* life, not restored to life as it was before. Children still young enough to be wowed by the 'new life' of large, bright sunflowers that have grown from dried-up seeds once buried in the ground, or the 'new life' of butterflies emerging from their entombment as chrysalis, might grasp more than we think.

 The story

See notes on storytelling materials on page 20.

You will need:
* The story basket
* The sand-coloured story cloth
* A basket of bricks, enough to make the base of a house
* A wooden table
* A tomb (made of modroc or an arrangement of stones: see page 21)
* A large stone
* A free-standing cross, about 16cm high
* The figure of Jesus, the resurrected Jesus, six disciples, Mary Magdalene, and two angels

Setting up the story

(Bring out the story basket and create an air of mystery as you open it.) I wonder who or what our story is going to be about today? I wonder where our story will be? *(Lay out the sand-coloured story cloth.)*

Here are some bricks. *(Take out the basket of bricks.)* What might these be for? *(After talking about some suggestions, make the base of a house near you.)* Is there something to go in this house? *(Take out the table and place it in the house.)* What might people do at this table?

What else? What's this? *(Take out the cross.)* I wonder how this will be part of our story? *(Lay the cross down in the space to the right of the story cloth.)*

Is there something in the story basket to go there? *(Bring out the tomb or make the tomb with stones.)* I wonder what this might be? It's got a way in and a way out… I wonder what might go in here? Perhaps our story will tell us.

(The house, cross and tomb form a triangle on the story cloth. When they are in place, sit back and view the cloth.)

So… a house with a table, a cross, and a kind of cave. *(Touch or point to the different parts as you remind children of the features.)* I think we've got everything we need to start. Are you ready for our story?

Telling the story

Once there was a man who was just like God. His words were like God's words, his thoughts were like God's thoughts and everything he did was what God would have done. This man was Jesus. *(Take Jesus from the story basket and rest him on the palm of your hand.)*

Wherever he went, lots of people wanted to come near to him. But Jesus had some special friends who were with him most of the time.

Jesus and his friends were happy when they were together. *(Place Jesus at the table and, as you are speaking, add his friends, including the figure for Mary Magdalene, placing them around the table.)* They talked together, they laughed together, and they ate meals together.

But something very sad was happening. Some people did not like all the things Jesus was doing and saying. One night, when Jesus had gone out to pray *(move Jesus away from the house, along the road towards the cross)*, some soldiers came and got hold of him. They took him away, and later, Jesus was fastened to a cross and left to die. *(Place Jesus in front of the cross.)*

His special friends were very sad. *(Line up the disciples outside the house as if looking at the cross.)* They couldn't be with Jesus any more. They couldn't talk with Jesus, they couldn't laugh with Jesus, and they couldn't eat meals with Jesus. They were very sad.

But even though Jesus was dead, some of his friends still wanted to look after him. They gently took his body down from the cross, carried him and laid him in a tomb. *(Hold Jesus carefully and move him along the road and place him in the tomb. Do not worry about trying to move any other figures here, as the movement becomes too complicated.)*

They covered the entrance and left him there where it was quiet and peaceful. *(Put the stone across the entrance.)*

But then something amazing happened. Some time later, we don't quite know when and we don't know how, God raised Jesus to new life. The large stone was moved *(move the stone to one side)* and Jesus came out of the tomb. *(Bring out the 'earthly' Jesus and replace immediately with the resurrected figure of Jesus. Return the figure for the 'earthly' Jesus to the basket: stand the figure of the resurrected Jesus a little way from the tomb.)* He wasn't dead any longer, but had new life. Listen again: God had raised Jesus from being dead to new life!

Early on the Sunday morning, Mary Magdalene, one of Jesus' special friends, went to the tomb. She still thought Jesus was dead. *(Move Mary along the road from the house to the tomb.)* She saw that the large stone had been moved away. She stood crying, not knowing what had happened to Jesus.

As she bent over to look into the tomb, she saw two angels. *(Place two angels in the entrance to the tomb.)* They asked her why she was crying and Mary said, 'They have taken away my Lord's body! I don't know where they have put him.'

Then Mary turned around *(turn the figure around)* and saw someone standing nearby. *(Move Jesus closer.)*

Mary Magdalene thought he was the gardener. She said, 'If you have taken his body away, please tell me, so I can go and get him.'

The man just said, 'Mary!' He called her by name. And when Mary heard her name, she knew his voice. 'Rabboni,' she said, which, in her language, means 'My great one'.

(Move Mary closer to Jesus.) Mary wanted to hug Jesus, but Jesus said, 'Don't hold on to me! But tell my brothers that I am going to the one who is my Father and my God, as well as your Father and your God.'

Mary Magdalene went to tell their friends that she had seen Jesus *(move Mary back along the road from the tomb to the house, and stand her in front of the other disciples)*, and she told them everything that Jesus had said to her.

(A storytelling hint: be open about the way you exchange the figure for the earthly Jesus with the figure for the resurrected Jesus. If you try to do it by sleight of hand and without the children seeing, you are likely to be 'rumbled' and then they will think that you are playing a trick. This is not how we want them to think of the resurrection.)

Talking about the story

✪ Talk about which part of the story the children liked best.

✪ Was there anything they did not like?

✪ Where would they like to be in the story? *(If possible, have a basket of spare figures so that they can put themselves in the story.)*

 Prayer

If you are doing this story in spring time, talk about the signs of new life around.

Dear Jesus, thank you for all the signs of new life around, for... Thank you that God raised you to new life and now you live with us, even though we cannot see you. Amen

 Reproduced with permission from *Praise and Play!* published by BRF 2009 (978 1 84101 563 7) www.barnabasinchurches.org.uk

Individual craft activity

A 'new life' Easter garden

For each child you will need:
* A tinfoil flan dish with straight sides
* A section of an egg box (for the tomb)
* A large stone
* Some small stones
* A cross made from two pieces of a craft stick, glued together at the intersection
* Soil or potting compost, packets of cress seeds and clippings from branches of fir trees

Place the egg box section near the edge of the tinfoil dish. Put soil in the tinfoil dish and over the egg box section. The soil needs to be deep enough for the cross to stand up in it. Make a path of small stones leading to the 'tomb'. Place the large stone across the entrance to the 'tomb'. Stand the cross in the soil. Stand the tree clippings in the soil. Scatter cress seeds. Explain to the children that they should keep the soil moist and watch what happens. Within a few days, the cress seeds will grow and bring new life to the garden.

Group craft activity

An Easter card to 'send' to the church

Fold a sheet of A3 card in half. On the front of the card, write or print a message such as 'A happy Easter to everyone'. On the inside, write or print, 'With love from everyone at Praise and Play.' Pre-cut flowers, flower centres and leaves (see template on page 72).

To make the card, ask each person to make a flower by gluing a flower centre on to the middle of a flower shape and two leaves behind the flower so that they overhang the edge. Ask everyone to stick their flowers on to the front of the card (or inside if extra space is needed).

Snack time

Shredded wheat nests

Melt some chocolate in a bowl in a microwave. Crumble up shredded wheat and coat it in the chocolate. Put the nests into paper cake cases and decorate with mini eggs on the top. Explain that nests and eggs are signs of new life that we can see around Easter time.

NB: Be aware of food allergies, especially wheat and milk.

Jesus is with us all the time

Bible reference: Acts 1:6–14 and 2:1–4

The Acts of the Apostles is generally considered to be the second book in a two-part work written by Luke. In his Gospel, Luke tells of the birth, life and ministry of Jesus throughout Galilee and Judea, culminating with his death and resurrection in Jerusalem, the centre of the Jewish world. In Acts, Jesus' continuing mission (in the hands of the apostles) begins in Jerusalem and ends in Rome, the centre of the then-known world. The two particular passages included in this session tell the story of Jesus' ascension into heaven and the coming of the Holy Spirit at the feast of Pentecost.

Let's explore further...

Jesus' ascension to heaven is not an easy concept for us to grasp. For 40 days the risen Jesus had appeared to his disciples at different times and in different situations, but it was perhaps inevitable that such appearances would cease. Although the 'earthly' Jesus' work occurred in a particular place and at a particular time in history, Jesus' mission was much greater than that. Jesus had to return to heaven so that he could be with everyone—in every place and in every age.

Before Jesus ascended into heaven, he charged the disciples with an important commission. They were to tell everyone in the known world about Jesus and all that he had done and said. The disciples were not going to have to do this in their own strength: Jesus promised them that the Holy Spirit would give them the power to fulfil this charge (Acts 1:8).

The feast of Pentecost was one of three highly significant festivals celebrated by people of the Jewish faith (the other two being the festival of Passover in the spring and the festival of Tabernacles in the autumn). At the feast of Pentecost, people remembered the time when, through Moses, God had given the Law to their ancestors on Mount Sinai. Many people, from many countries, came to Jerusalem to celebrate the feast of Pentecost, which explains the presence in Jerusalem of people from so many different countries at the time of the coming of the Holy Spirit (Acts 2:9–11). The streets of Jerusalem would have been teeming with people.

The coming of the Holy Spirit is perhaps one of those biblical passages where words cannot express adequately the enormity of the experience. Whatever the exact nature of the event, the result was that the disciples were transformed. Filled with the Holy Spirit, they had the vision, energy and commitment to fulfil the charge given them by Jesus.

So can it be said that this is a story for young children? Yes, but, although the events of Jesus' ascension and the coming of the Holy Spirit are a crucial part of the Christian story, we need to recognize that the account contains complex ideas for young children. In telling these stories, we are doing no more than laying down a first memory of these important events.

 **The story**

See notes on storytelling materials on page 20.

You will need:
* The story basket
* The sand-coloured story cloth
* Green fabric for the grass
* Bricks to create the base of a house
* A free-standing cross, about 16cm high
* A cloud, made from white felt
* The figures of the 'earthly' Jesus and the resurrected Jesus, figures for the disciples (placed in a small basket), people—both adults and children—also placed in a small basket

Setting up the story

(Bring out the story basket and create an air of mystery as you open it.) I wonder who or what our story is going to be about today? I wonder where our story will be? *(Lay out the sand-coloured story cloth.)*

Maybe it's not all sand. There's something green in the story basket. *(Take out the green fabric and place it on the far left of the sand-coloured story cloth.)* What could this be? *(Talk about possibilities. If desired, you could place a box lid or something similar under the green fabric to create a mountain effect.)*

There are some bricks in the story basket… what might these make? *(Make the base of a house on the right on the story cloth, nearer to you.)*

(Take out the cross.) There's something else here. Have you seen something like this before? What might it be? *(Place the cross in the middle of the story cloth and then sit back and view the story cloth.)*

So, some grass, a cross and a house. *(Touch or point to the different parts as you remind children of the features.)* I think we've got everything we need to start. Are you ready for our story?

Telling the story

Once there was a man who was just like God. His words were like God's words, his thoughts were like God's thoughts and everything he did was what God would have done. This man was Jesus. *(Take the Jesus from the story basket and rest him on the palm of your hand.)*

One day, something very sad happened. Jesus was fastened to a cross and he died. *(Take out the cross and hold Jesus against it.)*

But that wasn't the end of his story. Amazing things happened. Some people saw him alive in a new way. *(Take the figure of Jesus from the cross and replace it in the basket. Place the figure of the resurrected Jesus on the grass.)*

Then, when the time was right, Jesus met with his friends for the last time. *(Place the disciple figures around Jesus.)* Before he left them, Jesus made a promise. He said to his friends, 'You will receive power when the Holy Spirit comes upon you. And then you must tell people everywhere about all that I have said and done.'

When he had said this, Jesus was lifted up and a cloud took him out of their sight. *(Place cloud in front of Jesus and lift both Jesus and the cloud together, then return both items to the story basket.)*

The friends went back to the room where they were staying. *(Move the disciple figures to the house.)*

Some days later, a great wind from heaven filled the house, and all their hearts were filled with the Holy Spirit, just as Jesus had promised.

The friends were so excited, and they felt so strong, that they went out to tell people everywhere all the amazing things that Jesus had done and said. *(Move the disciples to different places on the story cloth.)* More and more people became friends of Jesus and were baptized. *(Bring out the basket of people and start to set them down, children and adults, near each of the disciples.)*

More and more people became friends of Jesus, and so Jesus' Church began—people who gathered together because they all wanted to be Jesus' friends and to live more like he lived. *(Gather the figures around the cross in the middle of the story cloth.)*

(If you have enough figures, you could invite everyone to place a figure down to add to the group of people.) And now we, too, are part of Jesus' Church and part of this great family of people, who are all Jesus' friends and want to live more like he lived.

Talking about the story

✪ Talk about which part of the story the children liked best.
✪ Was there anything they did not like?
✪ Do they know someone else who would like to be part of this great family, Jesus' Church? *(If you have enough figures, you could invite them to place a figure down for the person they are thinking of.)*

Prayer

Talk about anyone they know who might like to be part of Jesus' Church.

Dear Jesus, thank you that we can be part of your Church. Thank you that you are with us, even though we cannot see you. Amen

Individual craft activity

Stained glass windows

For each child you will need:
* An A4 acetate sheet, with a simple line drawing of the risen Jesus (see template on page 73)
* An A4 rectangular frame made from coloured card
* Torn pieces of tissue paper
* A message label saying, 'Jesus is with us all the time'
* A hanging thread
* Glue sticks and a hole punch (for the group as a whole)

Glue pieces of tissue paper on to the reverse side of the acetate sheet. Try not to leave any gaps. Glue the frame on to the right side of the acetate sheet. Glue the message label to the frame. Punch a hole in the middle of the top side and attach the hanging thread.

Group craft activity

A photo montage of your church

This activity is designed to encourage the idea that the church is the people, rather than just the building. In advance, ask everyone to bring in a photograph of themselves. Draw an outline of your church and ask everyone to stick their photograph inside the outline (you may need to trim some of the photographs first).

You could make this a whole-church activity by asking people from the worshipping community to add their photographs.

Snack time

Cloud biscuits

Bring white marshmallow biscuits and suggest to the children that white marshmallow reminds us of clouds. Chat about the fact that Jesus was taken up into a cloud when he went back to heaven.

NB: Be aware of food allergies.

Templates

Session 1

Figures of Mary, Joseph and baby in the manger

Session 2

Star

Session 3

Fish tail and fins

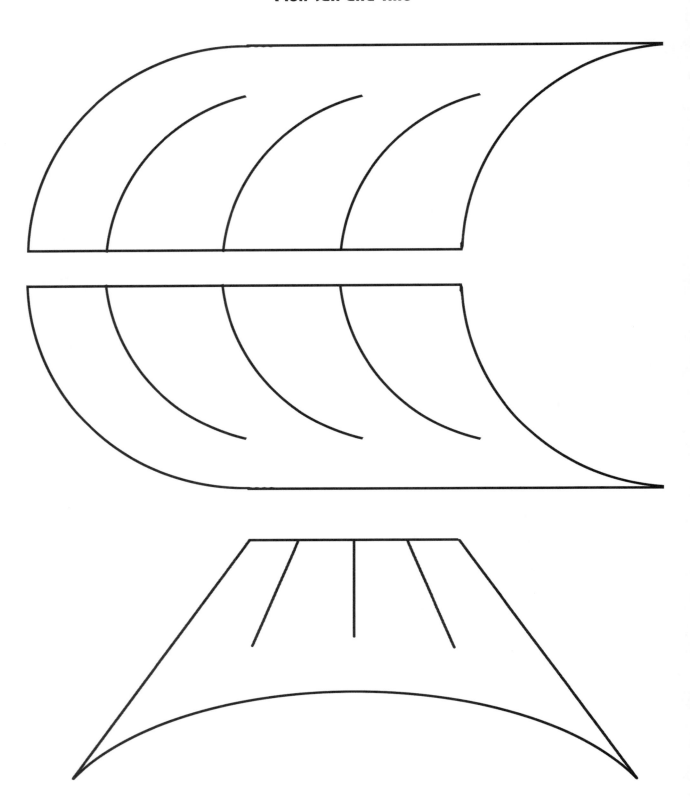

Sessions 4 and 7

Shepherd and sheep

Session 6

Puppet figure

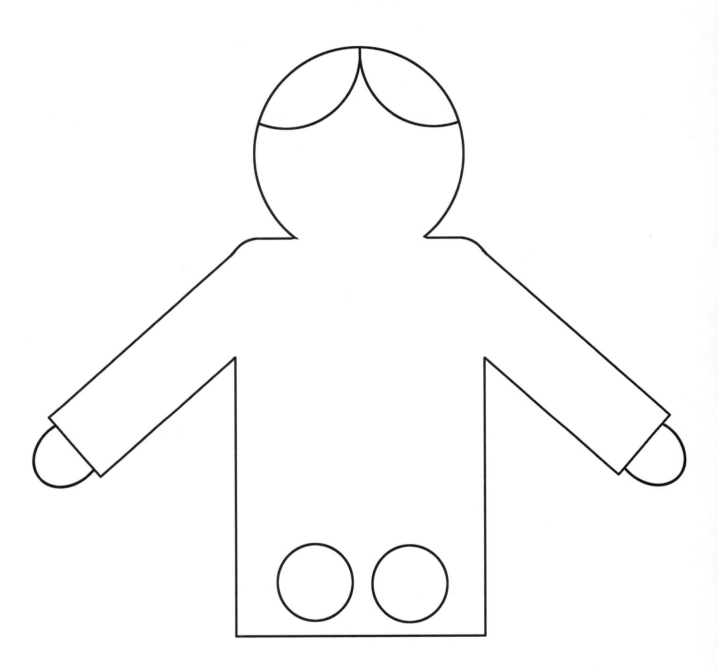

Session 8

Sail, mast, boat and handle

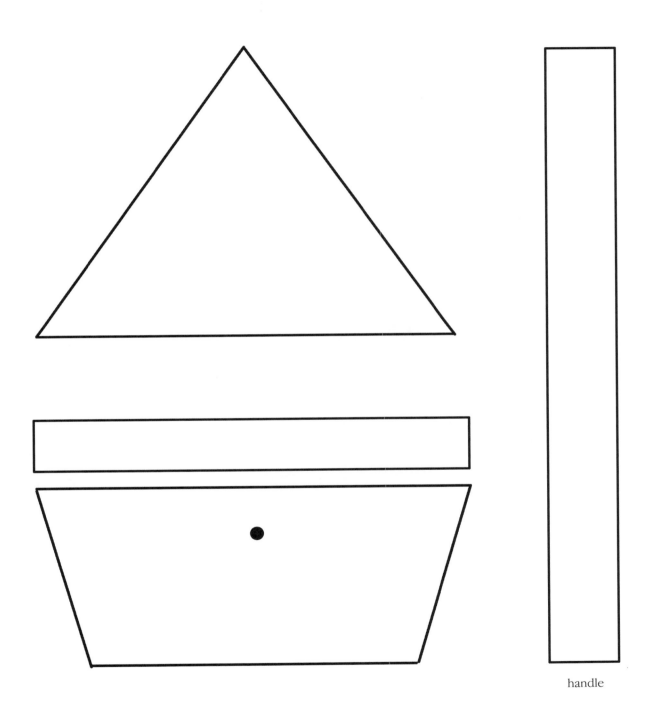

handle

Session 9

Basket, loaf and fish

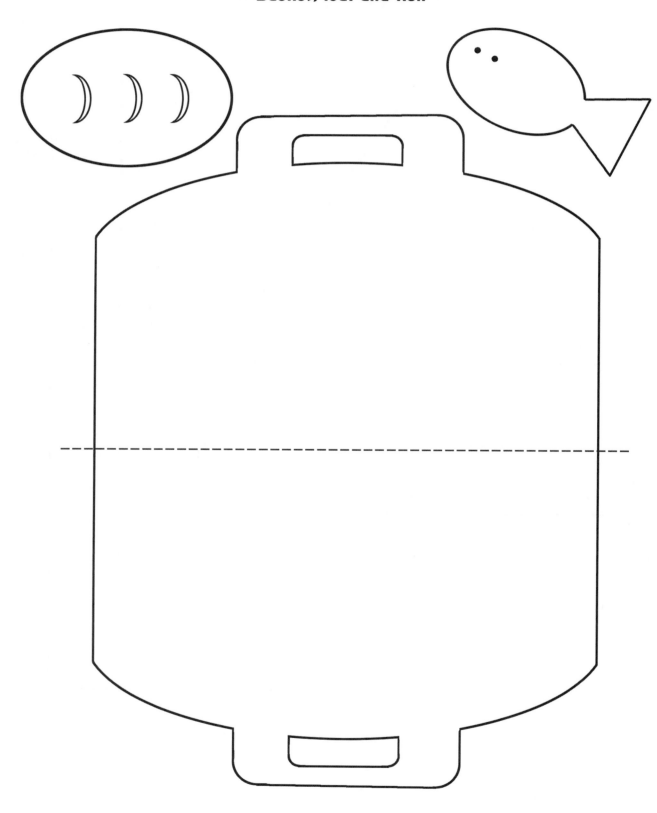

Session 10

Tree, trunk and leaf

folded edge

folded edge

Session 11

Flower shape, centre and leaf

Session 12

The risen Jesus

Bibliography

Songbooks

Come and Praise: Beginning, Jo Daykin (BBC Education)

Music CDs

Come and Praise: Beginning (2 CDs) (BBC Education)
God's Wonderful World, Julia Plaut (Kingsway Music)
Thank You, God, for Snails, Julia Plaut (Kingsway Music)
I Know Jesus Loves Me, Ishmael (Children's Ministry)

Resource books

Christmas Make and Do, Gillian Chapman (Barnabas, 2004)

Websites

www.seeandknow.com
www.tts-group.co.uk
www.mjjeducation.com